FAMILY TIME

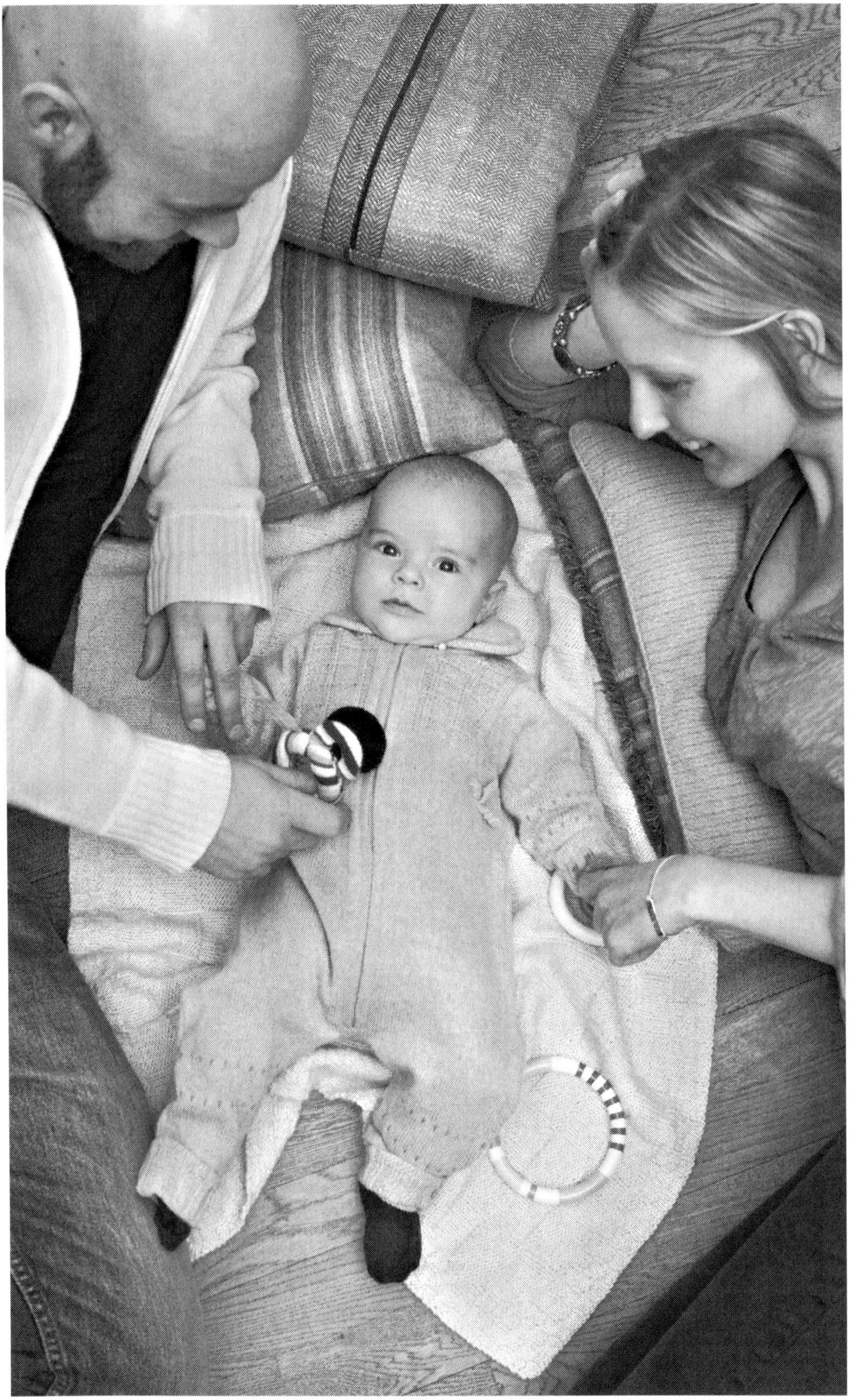

FAMILY TIME

Jesper Juul • Monica Øien

Photography: Marcel Leliënhof

family/lab

authorHOUSE

AuthorHouse™
1663 Liberty Drive
Bloomington, IN 47403
www.authorhouse.com
Phone: 1-800-839-8640

© 2012 by Jesper Juul. All rights reserved.

No part of this book may be reproduced, stored in a retrieval system, or transmitted by any means without the written permission of the author.

www.jesperjuul.com
www.family-lab.com
www.artofsayingno.tv
www.familylab.com.au

Other English titles:

Your Competent Child, published by Balboa Press
Your Competent Child DVD at www.textalk.se

English titles published by AuthorHouse:

Family Life
Here I am! Who are you?
No!

Translation: Hayes van der Meer

Published by AuthorHouse   10/12/2012

ISBN: 978-1-4772-2599-8 (sc)
ISBN: 978-1-4772-2598-1 (hc)
ISBN: 978-1-4772-2597-4 (e)

Any people depicted in stock imagery provided by Thinkstock are models, and such images are being used for illustrative purposes only.
Certain stock imagery © Thinkstock.

Because of the dynamic nature of the Internet, any web addresses or links contained in this book may have changed since publication and may no longer be valid. The views expressed in this work are solely those of the author and do not necessarily reflect the views of the publisher, and the publisher hereby disclaims any responsibility for them.

CONTENTS

Foreword ix

A house full of emotions 1

The bedroom 24

The baby's room 44

The child's room 67

The teenager's room 113

The bathroom 149

The kitchen 167

The living room 191

A final word 215

Thank you to the models:
Marie Elvira og Øystein, Fride, Teodor og Tevje,
Eldar og Alma, Hedda, Chris og Matheo,
Sara, Wilma, Margrete, Egil, Helene og Amalie,
Elise, Frida, Max, Aksel og Oscar.

Thanks to Polarn O. Pyret, www.polarnopyret.no
and Lille Lam, www.lillelam.no for the use of clothes.

FOREWORD

It is the middle of June and I am in the little Croatian village of Poreč near the Adriatic Sea. The temperature has reached a very comfortable 32°C/90°F and everything is lush and green, the birds are singing and the lizards are scurrying around the flower bed. I am sitting on a balcony with the well-spoken and highly experienced family therapist, Jesper Juul.

I am a producer, journalist, lecturer, mother, bonus mother and partner. My partner and I live with three boys: my own son Max who is 13 years old and my partner's two sons Carl Frederik who is 14 and Johan who is 11.

I want to produce a *conversation book* for parents and bonus parents. With this book I will be able to satisfy my curiosity and answer some of the many questions I have as a mother, parent and someone who lives in the modern world. I hope to answer some of the questions that I have struggled with for years. How can parents find out what is right and wrong in relation to raising children? Are we supposed to be guided by morality, religion, social ideology or the most popular trend of the day? Why are we told it is important to set limits? When do children have to go to bed? How do we as parents relate to teenage parties, sexual development, independence, desires and obsessions?

Jesper and I begin our conversation by navigating our way through a typical family home. A home where every room has its own functions and brings about different emotions. Inside the rooms we meet ourselves and those we live with. But why in these daily interactions do we repeat so much of what we dislike about our own upbringing. With a bit of luck we notice this and try to change our otherwise set ways of doing things. We are confronted by our less fortunate aspects through interactions with our partner and children. Hopefully, we will also be able to acknowledge the good things we do and celebrate these.

Just a few hours into my conversation with Jesper I realize that it is not possible to divide a family's life up into separate rooms—neither is it easy to divide our children's lives into age groups or phases. We meet similar challenges whenever our children are four months old or teenagers. This is especially true when it comes to closeness, leadership and authenticity. This also applies to our most loving partnerships. Are we able to have enough deep and meaningful conversations with those we love? Are we paying them enough attention? Are we present in a manner that they notice? What about the way we use our words—do others understand what we mean or would we benefit from taking a pause and carefully consider what it is we wish to share? Things can so easily go wrong if we constantly say "you" when speaking with others—especially our children. They will feel that they are the cause of the problem. If we stop defining others and instead become more personal our conversations will have a less critical nature and we are able to focus on the issues at hand.

Family Time

> *It is not what you say but how and why you say it that matters. This is the key to good and constructive communication within the family.*

Again and again Jesper stresses the importance of "striking while the iron is *cold*." We need to wait until things have calmed down before we talk about what has happened. Is this the easiest way to avoid misunderstandings and painful arguments? It is not *what* you say but *how* and *why* you say it that matters. This is the key to good and constructive communication within the family. Jesper encourages us to carefully consider what we do and then do it enthusiastically, authentically and be brave. This requires parental leadership. It is as simple as this: your family's happiness depends on your personal happiness. This is so because people around you become happy and content when you are.

I have read most of Jesper's books. I have been inspired, fascinated and challenged but most of all I have been surprised . . . So much of what he writes and speaks about has worked well in my daily life. It is absolutely possible to modify old patterns and negative behavior. I trust that this book will inspire you to relate and interact genuinely and lovingly with the people you love the most.

Monica Øien

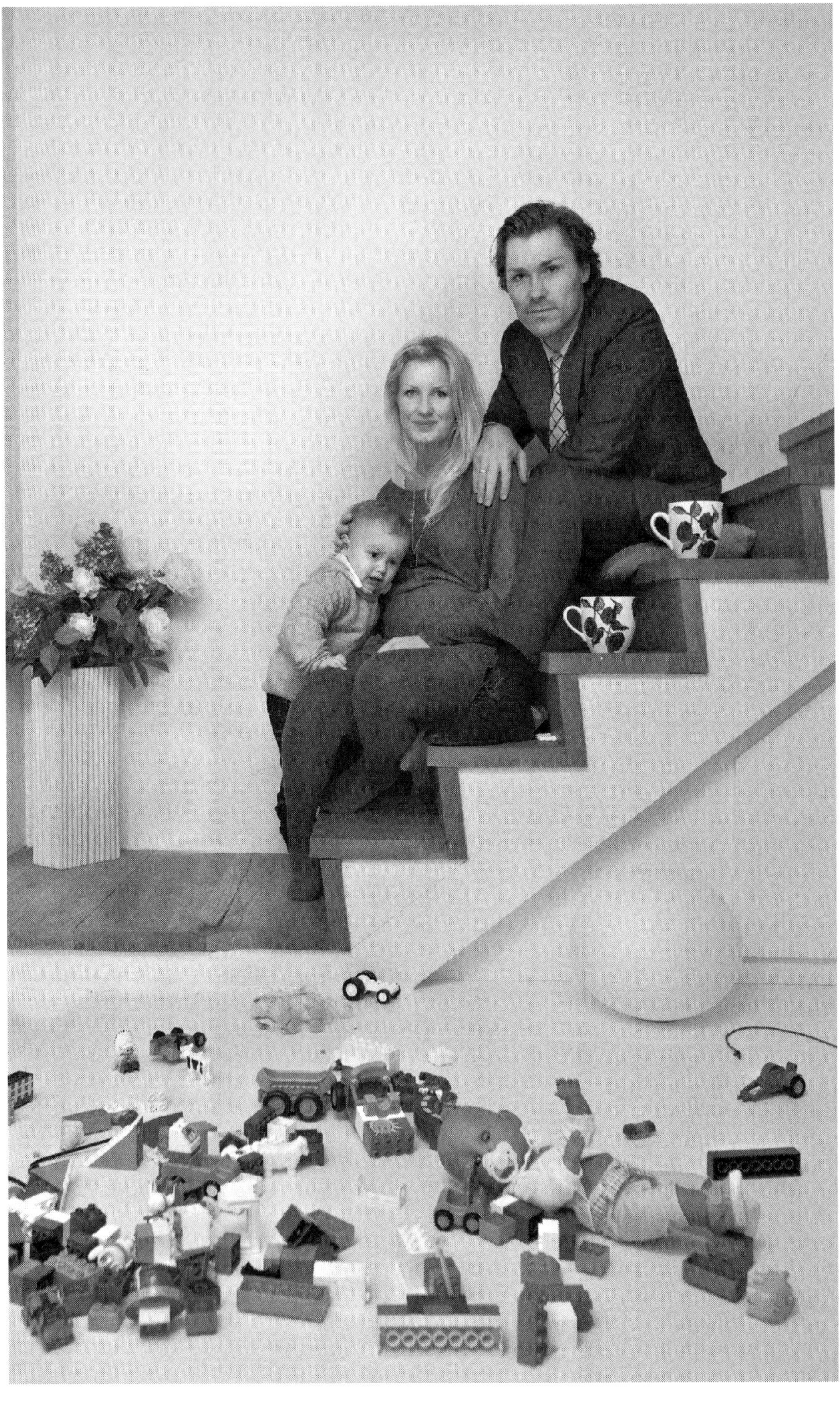

A HOUSE FULL OF EMOTIONS

What does it mean to be a nuclear family?

Going through somebody's front door and looking inside their home might be a good place to find an answer. This is the place that binds the family together. It is the physical space where older and younger people live. It is where different areas create space for play, sleep, work, growth, love, sex, food and much more. I wonder what is inside the home? Is it a nuclear family? Is the place full of atmosphere? Is it a space where the family spends time, lives and loves?

Every home has its own distinct atmosphere and personality. The values of your family reflect the people who live there—with their habits, social status and professions. What do we see when we enter the different rooms? What are the routines and experiences of those who live there? And what happens when we move from one room to another?

MONICA:
—*I suppose we usually think about a home as a place where a nuclear family lives. The mother and father are together and live with their shared children. Everything is peaceful and everyone lives in harmony with each other? Is that what "nuclear" means?*

JESPER:
—The family home needs to be put into a historical perspective. We may have made a mistake during the women's liberation movement in 1970s. I believe that the role of women back then was mistakenly defined as being predominantly functional. Seeing the role in that light had serious shortcomings and limitations which meant that we failed to see the most important contribution made by women, namely to create *atmosphere* or *"ambiance"* as the French eloquently put it.

Regardless of who does the housework, whether it is the man, woman or the children, the resulting atmosphere will be the most important aspect of the home. Consequently, it becomes something of an issue when people start hiring cleaners, ordering take-away and having their houses designed by interior designers. It might all look beautiful and the place might function really well but what about the atmosphere? The question is: "Whose atmosphere is it really?" Don't get me wrong, it is wonderful to have a house that is clean, well-organized, neat and tidy but deep down we know that this isn't enough. If we don't put our heart and soul into the things we do they remain exactly like that—just things!

The moment you enter someone's house you know if it is a real home or simply a place where people live. The latter often happens when people are busy. If both parents work outside of the home, the household and the family might, as a matter of course, become some kind of operation where things have to be organized and planned in advance—much like a project. This situation is inescapable when the logistics have to run like clockwork but for the children this is not enough. They require something completely different. It is important for them that there is a distinct difference between their home and their childcare or school. This difference narrows when the family functions mostly as an operation. The children will not thrive. They will be stressed and unhappy. If this pattern continues over a period of perhaps seven or eight years then the relationship between the parents will also suffer. Adults simply become spectators to each other's lives when they are primarily occupied with practical issues. The first symptom is often that the bedroom becomes a place where the bed is used just for sleep.

It is wonderful to have a house which is clean, well-organized, neat and tidy but deep down we know that this isn't enough. If we don't put our heart and soul into the things we do they remain exactly like that—just things!

When we look at the statistics we know that most children grow up in so-called *nuclear families* (at least for the first eight to nine years of their lives). There are also many one-parent families and stepfamilies where children have what we call *bonus parents*. Furthermore, people grow older these days, so "till death us do part" stretches over a much longer period than it did just a few generations ago.

Nowadays, a decisive prerequisite of a relationship is that it makes sense. It can be rocky, calm or any kind of relationship as long as it enriches our lives. If it does not, then we might as well be on our own. It is a fairly recent condition that a relationship must enrich our lives. Perhaps it is also the one that has the greatest impact on our family life.

—Well, if we hope to find the "one and only" who is the right person and with whom we will go through thick and thin then the traditional relationship is the ideal, isn't it?

—This is true. But reality is that many adults are likely to go through several long-lasting relationships—with or without children. This could give the impression that couples separate at the drop of a hat. In some cases this might be so but it is my experience that people take separation and divorce very seriously indeed—especially when children are involved. I don't think the deciding factor is the amount of conflicts or arguments. The question is rather whether the relationship is meaningful or not.

—How meaningful does it have to be? Many people have high expectations and the list to tick is very long. We can't expect the relationship to be meaningful 24/7 . . . ? We have to work hard at it, don't we?

—I completely agree. Meaningful doesn't mean constant harmony and total happiness. For a relationship to be meaningful it has to be enriching in a way that challenges you to grow as a person. Some of these challenges often take us by surprise and we might not feel particularly comfortable when they appear. This is the way it is with any loving relationship between two adults and between parents and children.

> *"Meaningful" doesn't mean constant harmony and total happiness. For a relationship to be meaningful it has to be enriching in a way that challenges you to grow as a person.*

The fact that our relationships must enrich our personal lives is a new phenomenon. Our grandparents didn't think like that at all. Add to this the fact that there is a distinct difference between what we believe is meaningful. Some believe personal challenges are meaningful whilst others, often men, find peace and calm meaningful. For many, if not most, the symbol of success becomes *harmony*. How this is achieved obviously differs from family to family.

Many people write to FamilyLab asking how much pain they must endure and how long they need to work on their problems before they give up. It goes without saying that any kind of loving relationship needs to endure a certain amount of pain. If the pain however, isn't followed by something positive—a realization, an insight or some kind of development—but is repeated month after month, then it will be meaningless pain. This is something we have to work on and preferably improve on, because we are talking about an intimate relationship with another person whom essentially we don't really know.

—It seems possible to feel a sense of loneliness even though we are in a relationship. Often this is because one partner doesn't display any kind of understanding—at least this is what the other person experiences.

—A female client once said to me: "Jesper, I have two options: either I live with a man or I live wanting one." She was part of the first generation to acknowledge that marriage wasn't a social necessity. Her generation realized that marriage is an existential choice. She did not want to live with a man who didn't enrich her life on a fundamental level.

—So . . . is the ideal family a family without conflicts?

—No, not at all! We must remember that a conflict is simply a situation when two people have two different needs or desires. Nevertheless, conflicts are far too often considered as difficult and negative. This stems from the days when the family was a hierarchical and totalitarian structure. We know that a totalitarian system doesn't like conflicts whereas a democratic system has to live with them. These days of course, there is not one cultural or moral way of doing things. As a consequence every single family has to search for their own ways. Many find comfort when something is presented as a "truth". For example, when it was found that breast-feeding was best for both mother and baby we suddenly witnessed young intelligent mothers bullying those who didn't breast-feed—they were seen as bad mothers because they didn't follow the "truth" of the day. It is the exact same pattern we see in relation to divorce. During some periods it is generally accepted—then suddenly it isn't. It is a great pity that our society doesn't seem to have much room for these often complex situations. I don't believe it is possible to find answers to everything but if we search for them, I am sure we can find some kind of meaning.

—*Do the solutions and answers come to us when we are older . . . ?*
Along the way it is all about being alert, meeting the challenges, forgiving what can be forgiven and finding growth wherever we can.

—Most of our norms and values were developed during a period of time when there was a shortage of material things. We are not geared for, and don't really know how to, live in an affluent society. I have heard many people being critical and condemning the fact that children become consumers at a very early age. I am not too concerned because that is the world they live in—and so do their parents. Besides, I am confident that sooner or later the trend will turn. It is the way history progresses. The big question is whether or not we take note and learn from all this.

Statistically speaking, a high percentage of marriages end in divorce. My partner and I separated when our son was 12 months old. Most of the time he lives with me and then has extended weekends with his father. It works for us. It is what he knows and is natural for him. The challenge comes when one of us meets a new partner and wishes to live with that person. Maybe the new partner will even have his or her own children. That is when the situation changes dramatically because our son is forced into living with people he hasn't chosen to live with.

—How does a bonus parent relate to this new family set-up and to the children in that new family?

—Children will not automatically accept being brought up by people they are not related to. They are able to reject this when they are just two years old as well as when they are 13. From the outset, if bonus parents behave as if they are family then there will be no family at all. This is a paradox not many parents think through.

Becoming a bonus parent is all about creating relations with the new children—it is obviously not about becoming equals but to work out whether or not there is a basis for joining each other's families.

When we, as adults, fall in love we are greatly supported by chemistry and hormones. After a period of four to five years it becomes evident whether or not we will also be lifelong friends. When it comes to children however, it doesn't work like that. First they will become friends and not until that happens will they work out whether or not they want to become family. I have met many families who separated while the children were very young. The parents soon met new partners and the children love their bonus parents but not until the age of five of six did they ask if they could call them "mother" or "father". It took a long time for them to confirm that the friendship had matured and they were ready to become family.

—*If you are in a relationship with your second or third partner you might have a slightly different approach to things. Most likely, you are more mature and more experienced. Inevitably, this will have some influence on the children. Some become curious and might want to know if their parent has sex with the bonus parent. How do you answer them?*

—I think you should say: "Yes!"—that is, if you do have sex. It has always been difficult for children to imagine that their parents have sex with each other. I am not sure why this is so. Teenagers think it is embarrassing but the question arises because they are philosophizing about life. They think about sex in the exact same way as when they ask their parents what happens when they die. So don't worry too much about it. Besides, they forget the answer as soon as they hear it. Sex is part of children's lives and part of the world they live in. Obviously, they think about it and you will be able to share something very precious with them if you are able to help them understand that sex can be beautiful. The sex that they see or hear about in public is often very problematic.

—*In many countries homosexual couples have gained the same rights as heterosexual couples. They can marry and have the right to apply for adoption or have children through IVF. Different types of family structures are emerging. We know that some adopted children have a strong desire to meet their biological parents. What are your thoughts about families where children grow up with two parents of the same gender where they might never be able to meet their biological parents?*

—It is my experience that it makes absolutely no difference for the children whether they live with parents who have a homosexual or a heterosexual relationship. I have had more than a hundred homosexual couples in therapy, men as well as women. The fundamental mechanisms are exactly the same. From the children's perspective I have absolutely no hesitations about a homosexual couple adopting. There is no research that indicates that they are worse parents or that it is detrimental to the children.

I do however, believe we made a mistake when we decided that having children was a human right. In many countries couples have a right to three IVF treatments. Children have become a "must-have". Some adults need another person who depends on them to feel they have personal value. This is fine as long as we remember that the child has exactly the same needs and rights, namely to know that they are valued by their parents other than as an essential accessory. I don't think everybody necessarily should become parents.

—Is this your general understanding, which includes heterosexual as well as homosexual couples?

—Yes absolutely!

There will always be people who are unable to conceive. Not long ago people had the children they could have and they didn't use preventative measures—not very effective ones anyway. Today, everyone can have one or several children—even those who perhaps shouldn't.

Once I met a man in San Francisco. He was around 70 years old, a monk and educated in the area of traditional Chinese medicine. One of his patients was my friend Ken Dychtwald who was hoping to have a baby with his wife, Maddy. After a couple of months she became very impatient. I went along with Maddy to the old Chinese man who said to me: "Mr. Jesper, I need your help, I cannot speak to Maddy and Maddy cannot listen to me, so if you please . . ." He then told me that Maddy couldn't conceive because: "Maddy *wants* baby too much. You must ask her to stop the treatment." Two years later they had their first naturally conceived baby and another one two years after that.

Whether or not it is possible to fall pregnant depends partly on the connection between body and soul. We all know stories of couples who try and try. Then they give up and apply for adoption. Soon after they conceive naturally.

It is not enough for the child to receive what we have to offer, we also have to be open to receive what the child has to offer. The good and the bad.

—*Should we leave it up to God or fate or whatever we might believe in?*

—Perhaps that might serve us better. I am not of a particular religious faith nor do I advocate any belief system. Politicians in the western world are telling us that we must produce more children to keep our economies growing. The pressure is on.

—*Having children is also a status symbol, isn't it?*

—It is an issue full of paradoxes. It is seen as a measure of success to have a child—if the child is healthy and well-functioning that is! On the other hand, it is also a measure of success if the parents—especially the mother—is unaffected by having had children. Life should preferably continue as if nothing happened. It is by no means my intention to offend those who wish to have children, I just need to stress that the relationship with a child must go both ways. It is not enough for the child to receive what we have to offer, we also have to be open to receive what the child has to offer. The good and the bad. If we are not ready for that, then it is probably better if we remain childless.

I grew up in the country. My grandmother was an artist and dressmaker. I would find a picture in a magazine of a dress I really liked, then she could make it for me. Within a few weeks she had created this beautiful dress and I was proud to go to the ball or birthday party. But I had to be patient. For weeks the dress would only exist in my dreams. Today, things are different. We have more money and can, by and large, buy the things we need and want. So I start to wonder what happened to gratefulness and humility.

—*Children are given things almost instantly and sometimes without much thought. This means they don't have the opportunity to experience the joy of anticipation. What happens to those who never develop the ability to wait for things?*

—They miss out on the excitement of waiting and looking forward to something. They don't learn about that wonderful experience. Instead they learn that every need and desire must be satisfied as soon as possible. For obvious reasons this can later lead to the need for them to subdue any frustration by the use of alcohol, drugs and medication. These days, many children are sheltered and protected from just about any feeling of loss, pain and frustration. They turn into some kind of Teletubbies. When children grow up like that it shouldn't be a surprise when they grow up feeling helpless and lost or they go to the extremes to be able to feel that they are in fact alive.

—*Is it our bad conscience because we are so busy or is it because of our unrealistic expectations that we end up buying so much stuff for them? As a sort of compensation?*

—Time pressures are self-imposed. Reality is that two working adults actually do have more spare time today than adults have ever had before. It is not so much about how much accumulated time we spend together but rather how much time we have once we are together. When you have been together for two or three hours and have finished talking about the things you have to talk about there might be silence for a little while. After that you will start saying things you haven't heard yourself say before. That is when it becomes personal and intimate. The conversations prior to that are usually just superficial or routine.

This is why so many people return from a holiday with a lot of new energy and a sense of closeness—or they return home and separate. When we initially fall in love with each other or a newborn arrives, much of what we say is just nonsense. Soon the daily routines kick in. These are filled with drop-offs and pick-ups, shopping, cooking and doing 50 million different things. Deep down we might be really interested in how the children are going but the way we find out often becomes some kind of interview. You will never find out who the other person really is, if all you get is answers. Add to this the risk that you might ask the wrong or inappropriate questions.

> *If you go hiking with your child for a few days he or she will start saying things spontaneously. You will hear things they themselves didn't realize were ready to be said. This is how we get to know each other.*

—*Conversation is what is needed!*

—Absolutely! If you go hiking with your child for a few days he or she will start saying things spontaneously. You will hear things they themselves didn't realize were ready to be said. This is how we get to know each other. Remember that silence is just as important as what is being said. It is interesting that it is easier for us to connect when we are at a restaurant than when we sit at home around the dining table. I travel a lot and I often eat out on my own. I can observe families and it is evident that the children love eating out. They have a really good time when their parents are able to focus on each other instead of them. It is really uncomfortable for a child to be at the centre of attention all the time.

It is uncomfortable for anyone to be at the centre of attention all the time. It can feel really invasive. It is as if someone takes something away from you—your personal space. When you are under the spotlight you do not feel safe enough to express yourself personally. I used to work with Dorthe Skappel from the Danish TV Channel TV2. She told me that she and her two daughters used to have a diary in the bathroom. In this book they could write about things that were on their minds—positive or negative. No one felt the need to comment about the things others wrote about. But they could quietly sit there and read—and write.

—We are often after instant answers, explanations and solutions. Perhaps this has the opposite effect. What do you think about such a diary? A place where we can quietly express our frustrations, joys and grief.

—It sounds like an excellent idea! I have often quoted an Israeli family therapist who said that we should "Strike while the iron is cold!" That is exactly what we need to do when there is a conflict. We can hardly ever solve a conflict while thunder is raging. It is a good idea to wait until things have calmed down.

Strike while the iron is cold!

If you would like an honest response from your child you need to say the following: "I would like to know the three worst things about me as a father—or mother." If there is mutual trust and openness between you it is possible that they will tell you two things. They might also want to tell you what is good about you but it is important that the negative things are said first, otherwise you will just be exchanging sweet nothings. Then you can ask what your child would like you to do about them. You can ask if he or she has any good ideas: "How can things improve at home? The summer holidays are coming up—what are we going to do?" This meeting could last for 30 or maybe 45 minutes—not for too long. Remember to thank your child for their help.

There are very few conflicts that are worth much time. That applies to conflicts between children and parents as well as between the parents themselves. Within the first 15 minutes everyone will have said everything that is important. After that it is just an argument where most sentences start with: "You . . . !" A great deal of our conflicts take a long time simply because we are so self-obsessed. We need to take time out and reflect. It is a good idea to be quiet and ask ourselves: "What is this conflict really all about? What is it I want out of it?"

It is typical for every family I have met that the *presence* of love is not enough—more is needed for things to function. Things don't just happen simply because we like or love each other. Not long ago most women would get angry when their partners were unable to operate as *mind-readers*. They thought: "If you love me then you must know what I need!" For thousands of years women have not been allowed to express what they wanted. All they could do was to hope that the men were able to work it out for themselves.

Love alone cannot keep a family together. Everyone needs to put in more than that.

Love alone cannot keep a family together. Everyone needs to put in more than that. If you are part of a step-family (or *bonus family*, as we prefer) then it is a good idea to schedule regular family meetings right from the beginning. What works and what doesn't? As adults we need to be open and let everyone speak—and make sure we listen.

—I guess it is also important that the children feel they are "heard" during these meetings even though they might not say much. How do you go about that?

—The children must know that it is just fine to say whatever is on their mind. Perhaps they need to be part of these family meetings for a few years before they raise their voices. Nevertheless, very young children will benefit from this just as teenagers will. No family is able to do this without some fine-tuning and practice.

These meetings are in fact also a good idea for couples. Turn off the phone and the TV three or four times per year. Or go away for a few days and talk about how the relationship is going and work out if anything needs to be changed. There is nothing as attractive as a person who exposes his or her soul. Our physical attractions are completely irrelevant. The mutual openness awakens the desire, very easily. When one partner asks: "Do you still love me?" what they are asking is really something entirely different, namely: "I would really like to be a valuable part of your life. Is that the way you see me? If so, I need to know what kind of value it is because I can neither hear or see it." We all have this very basic need to be valued by another person.

An excellent time to tell your child this is at a special celebration or anniversary. Say something like: "I have now lived with you for 14 years and I would like to share with you how this has enriched my life . . ."

I was put to the test a few years ago. My son who was 11 really wanted a computer game but he was far too young for that particular game. I asked Jesper how I could deal with this. He suggested that instead of just saying: "No!" I could ask my son to think about it for two days. I did this and during that time he had to think of some arguments both for and against buying it. When he came to me a few days later he had decided not to buy the game. This was a surprise to me, as I had expected the opposite.

—*It is difficult to work out how much the children should decide within the family. How much "family democracy" is appropriate?*

—Firstly, allow me to point out that family life has very little to do with democracy. In a democracy no one is completely satisfied. The idealistic values behind democracy are excellent but it is really all about distributing power and wealth. Within the family we have more power than money. I have often said that children should not decide everything but they must be taken seriously—their individualities, dreams and needs. If I want a healthy relationship then I must also take my partner seriously instead of judging him or her and decide what he or she can or cannot do. The ideas of individuality and the individual's value to society are relatively new concepts. Many fear that this will lead to individualism. Reality is that people who grow up learning to respect their individuality will function well socially. Those who become egocentric and lack empathy are the ones who have had their integrity violated and who have had little opportunity to develop a sense of self-worth.

Reality is that people who grow up learning to respect their individuality will function well socially. Those who become egocentric and lack empathy are the ones who have had their integrity violated and who have had little opportunity to develop a sense of self-worth.

I do not support the notion that children, first and foremost, should be obedient. Unfortunately, people's minds are geared in such a manner that we think in *opposites*. When I say children shouldn't necessarily be obedient, many assume that their disobedience is fine. This is far from the truth. I propose and recommend an alternative which is all about parents safeguarding their children's individuality and letting them take greater and greater responsibility for themselves.

We tend to underestimate children's abilities to fit in with what their parents are doing and how they are behaving. Children relate with equal importance to our conscious behavior as they do to our subconscious behavior—the things that happen between the lines. Parents do certain things but do not understand why their children don't respect them. If we observe what is going on, it quickly becomes evident that the parents are not actually doing what they think they are doing—or even intending to do. Instead of clearly saying: "No!" when their tired child asks to stay up and play, they say: "Perhaps it is time for you to go and lie down? Aren't you getting tired?" They leave it up to the child to interpret this vague message. Yet, the child is not able to do this as it requires an intellectual capacity which they do not yet possess. A three year old does not understand that her father doesn't want to be interrupted when he is on the phone if he says to her: "Right now I am on the phone!" Much of what parents call disobedience is in fact caused by parents not expressing themselves clearly or because parents do the opposite of what they think.

The logical consequence and outcome of a society built on freedom and democracy is that we must take personal responsibility for ourselves. This is not something we are taught at school—or anywhere else for that matter. The opposite of personal responsibility is conformity which many people experience as comforting. When we are afraid we seek refuge and by nature we feel comfortable with the familiar.

—*Is that good?*

—Conformity is good in the sense that it gives some kind of comfort but it is difficult to conform when there is no general consensus. Reality is that there isn't just *one* way of doing things these days.

No child anywhere in the world grows up without being negatively influenced by their parents. To hope that we can be perfect parents is absurd. The best parents a child can have are those who take responsibility for their mistakes. From time to time all of us are difficult to live with and those who try not to be difficult are even worse. People who always seek to compromise and do whatever they can to avoid conflicts have a very negative influence on the whole community as well as a detrimental impact on their own lives. The rest of the community will live with that person's need for compromise, thus becoming *enablers* and thereby feeding the *victim role*.

We are all self-destructive to some extent. This is part of our personality but we are rarely aware of it because of what I call our *strategy of survival*. This is an age-old instinct which we don't notice until our children arouse it because they challenge the core of our existence. They constantly challenge us and force us on a journey of personal growth—or they turn us into tyrants.

Family Time

In a partnership something similar happens. Either we grow and develop as people—or we become submissive or turn into bullies. In Europe it looks like these two groups are equal in size. One half believes relationships provide opportunities for personal growth by dealing with conflicts and getting on with life. The other half does whatever they can to avoid conflicts. I have met Spanish couples who believe life was better during the Franco regime because they didn't have to think or be responsible in the same way as they do now. An aspect of democracy is the need for us to make choices. This can in fact be very stressful because we have never been taught how to make choices—not at home or at school. We have to learn this and there are many who actually don't want to learn this. Their priorities are comfort, peace, quiet and ease of life. This is the masculine definition of family life: dad comes home from work and wants peace and quiet. These days we see this in a new format because men are less and less dictatorial. Many modern men submit and repress their own needs and desires, and succumb to the wishes of their partners. There will be no conflicts but after a few years the women become extremely frustrated because they have had to take on all responsibility. You see it in the shops: the man pushes the trolley and the woman has the shopping list. During the early days of their relationship she might ask him what he wants for dinner, to which most men would say: "I am not sure—what would you like?" She might ask him again so he changes his answer and says that it doesn't really matter to him. After a few years she realizes there is no point asking and simply puts whatever she wants in the trolley. She has become lonely as she isn't challenged.

To hope that we can be perfect parents is absurd. The best parents a child can have are those who take responsibility for their mistakes.

—Is it possible for parents to disagree about how to bring up their children and still do a good job?

—Absolutely! The idea that parents must agree on everything was important in the days when parents had to have complete power. There was no room for disagreement at the top. Such is the nature of all power. I have met thousands of couples and I have not yet met one couple who agreed on everything. I really do believe that there is a point in children having two parents: they have two because they need their differences to be able to develop their own personality.

Allow me to return to the subject of men not being able to take responsibility for themselves. As an example I shall use a conversation my wife and I have over and over again. We might be expecting friends or going out for the evening. A couple of hours before we leave, she comes and asks me what I think she should wear. I tell her what I think and a little while later she returns and, as expected, wears something completely different. All women understand the logic of this: knowing what other people think makes it easier for us to work out what we think. Many men have asked me why I bother telling her what I think when she doesn't follow my advice anyway. They turn it into a power struggle, yet that is not what it is about. Instead, it really should be a constructive interaction.

When you live with children for 18 years (or more) it is an immense benefit that the parents are different. It provides the children with opportunities to role model different people. It is also absurd when parents demand their children's grandparents implement and apply the same rules they have.

—The other day I was out shopping for clothes with my son. We found a shirt that I thought would be really nice for him. I told him so and asked if he would like something like that. While he was

looking through the different clothes he often came back to the shirt. "What would you like?" I asked him, "They have plenty of nice things!" He ended up buying the shirt I liked and I wonder if he did it to please me? What does an episode like this tell us about a child who really ought to challenge his parent's opinion and make his own choices?

—It tells me that he trusts you, and that he is a little bit insecure. You didn't focus on how easy the shirt would be to wash, the price or any of those kind of "mother" things. Your focus was on who he is, which made it possible for him to assess your suggestion. He probably thought: "She usually makes sensible decisions so I trust her point of view." When you tell him what you think he knows where you stand. If you don't tell him what you think because you are worried he will make up his mind just to please you, then he doesn't get the clarity he needs.

—*Children who grow up in families without limits, such as bed times, dinner routines, etc, will later tell you how they cried out for boundaries when they were children. Often their behavior tells you one thing but on the inside something different is happening. How can the parents find a balance?*

—You do that by being personal. Many parents of my generation tried to follow an ideology of some kind but they were never authentic. The problem with ideologies is that they in themselves will always be more important than the individual person. That generation found the idea more important than reality. Some adults focused on *liberty, equality and fraternity*. In reality though, this does not differ greatly from fundamentalist Christian thinking, which doesn't think much of the individual. Instead it requires unconditional conversion and submission. You are either in or you are out. What you, as a parent, need to do is get to know yourself with your partner and with your child. You need to find out what you want and don't want, and where your boundaries are instead of tormenting yourself with doubt about whether you are right or wrong.

I would like to share a story about a four year old boy who went to his father and asked: "What's the time?" He answers: "I am not sure, what do you think?" This is an example of what is called *anti-authoritarian* upbringing and is of course an unfortunate strategy. With an ongoing approach like that, children become lonely and depressed. It is very important for children that their parents have substance and are able to show character. This also applies when meeting an adult partner. You need a partner who is able to challenge you, and not just admire you and service your every need.

> *You need a partner who is able to challenge you, and not just admire you and service your every need.*

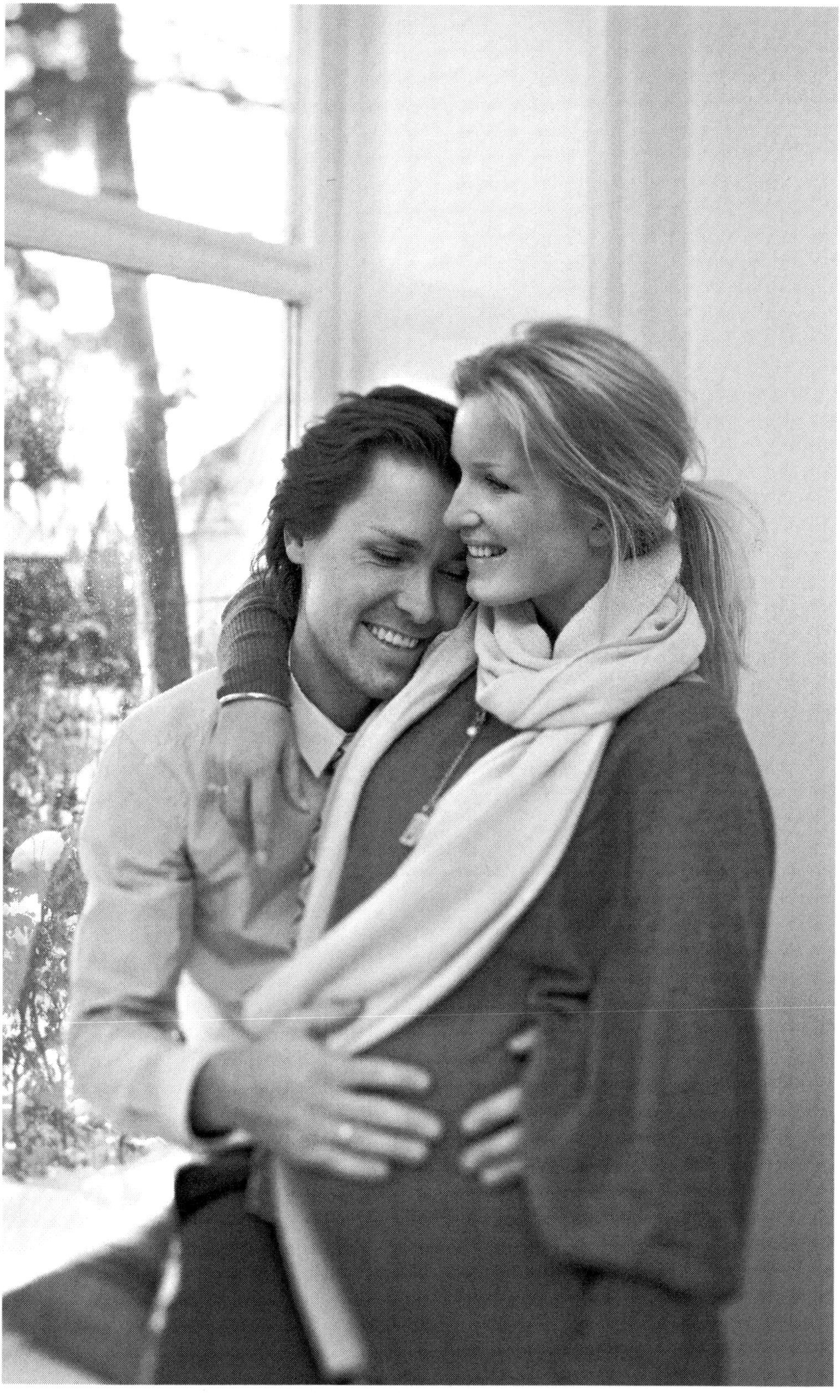

THE BEDROOM
– From two to three people

The transition from being partners to being parents is monumental. It is the phase in our lives which seriously puts our relationship to the test. We start looking at each other in a different light and begin seeing things through the eyes of the new baby. We are no longer just each others partners—now there is a new partner involved. And we become role models to the baby. Tension easily develops. How nice would it be to be just a little bit better prepared?

MONICA:
—The new baby will change the dynamics when the couple is no longer just a pair. How is the father going to relate to his partner when she suddenly prioritizes a different person ahead of him?

JESPER:
—The father's choices during the child's upbringing are vital no matter what he decides to do. If he chooses not to engage and has to spend time away during the first couple of years he will end up with a completely different family than if he hadn't. The mother

Family Time

will automatically and obviously assume a powerful position in relation to the child but also in relation to the father. He will have to learn to live with the fact that his child has assumed a higher priority in his partner's life than he has. It is evidently beneficial for the whole family when both parents can be equally involved with the upbringing.

Sooner, rather than later, the parents have to acknowledge that what they had together as a couple no longer exists. What they have now is something different. The dynamics change just like they do at work when someone resigns and new people begin. The couple can look at the situation and say that it is difficult. Alternatively, they can accept the fact that the old dynamics simply don't exist any longer and say: "Out with the old and in with the new!"

—*Don't parents also need to be able to be romantic lovers at times?*

—Sure, but they shouldn't do it just because they want to have what they used to have before the baby entered their lives. They should do it because they need it, want it and like it. The baby doesn't destroy the parent's relationship. This might happen as a result of the nostalgic memories which they dream of, but will never have again.

> *The baby doesn't destroy the parent's relationship. This might happen as a result of the nostalgic memories which they dream of, but will never have again.*

—*This could come as a shock to many—and bring a degree of sadness.*

—Yes, it is a loss. A tremendous loss. But try this: one evening about a month or so before your first baby is born you could get together—or maybe go away for a weekend and say: "Well, time has come for us to say goodbye to this relationship as we know it. Soon, we will have a completely different one." Most people don't find it easy to say: "Goodbye!" It is much easier saying: "See you later!" We really need to learn to say: "Goodbye!" and do so comfortably.

When we expect our first child most of us will have to say: "Goodbye!" to something which is really beautiful. We must give ourselves time to mourn this beautiful relationship which will cease to exist. Talk about your dreams as well as your frustrations. Only then will you be able to welcome the new family with all of your heart.

—What happens to the first born child who suddenly needs to relate to a new sister or brother?

—The outdated psychological theories suggest that child number one will be jealous when number two arrives. But it is not jealousy at all. The eldest just needs some guidance and learn how to mourn the loss of what once was. It comes without saying that number one has looked forward with excitement to having a sibling but he or she will soon realize that there is a down side to it as well. This is only natural. Number one will no longer have the feeling of being valued by the parents in the same way as before.

It is really difficult to guide the child through this loss. The father might take his child's hand and say: "What do you think about the little one who has arrived? I am really happy that she is here and she is so lovely. But sometimes I do think she is quite annoying. Don't you think so?" It will be such a relief for the eldest to have these feelings validated by the parents. He or she will no longer feel like an outsider within the family. It must be alright to feel that the arrival of a newcomer isn't only wonderful.

If parents were able to bid their relationship farewell then they will be much better at helping the eldest child when new siblings arrive.

In the past we used to resort to lecturing and saying: "You are the eldest child now. You should be sensible enough and not be mean to the little one." I still speak with parents who say this to their children. When that happens it will become even more difficult being the eldest brother or sister. If we instead let them know that it is alright to be frustrated with younger siblings the tension will disappear.

—*This sounds like a good idea for all projects we throw ourselves into.*

—Part of the journey of getting ready for a new relationship really does require that we say properly: "Goodbye!" to the old one. It is not too different from saying: "Goodbye!" to someone who dies. If you don't get a chance to express what that person has meant to you—good and bad—it really will be draining for you later.

If you have been betrayed by your partner you have the option of playing victim for the rest of your life or you acknowledge the truth: it takes two to enter a relationship and it takes two to split up. If both partners were thriving there would be no reason to split. When you are able to say: "Goodbye!" you take responsibility for your part of the separation.

—*If you however, stay together for a long time you will also go through highs and lows. Do different stages of a relationship have their own distinct challenges and crisis?*

—If you are together for long enough you may experience a series of three so-called *seven-year itches*.

The *first itch* comes about because we have said: "Yes!" too often and because we have forgotten to think of ourselves as distinctly different and unique individuals. Instead we often use the 3rd person description: *we*. By inference we include our partner when speaking because we become "joined at the hip" as it were. We no longer speak for ourselves but on behalf of each other. We really need to untangle ourselves and rediscover that *you* and *I* are two individuals. So we must clarify our expectations and desires the way each of us individually sees them.

The *second itch* is all about the realization that we are going to live together until we grow old. "If she doesn't change, do I still want to live with her when I turn 70?" In this case it is important to acknowledge who the person you are with really is. Not your own personal illusions or hopes. A woman once asked me: "Do you think that deep down my husband is alright?" I said that I did think so. To which she replied: "I know that! It is just that I am tired of spending my life walking around in a diving suit." That was well said because she clearly had enough of trying to interpret what he meant and trying to find out who he was. She felt she had to look for her husband deep down on the "bottom of the sea".

During the *third itch* we will ask a new question: "Do I really want this—for the rest of my life?" It has to be noted that this question not only refers to the relationship but relates to work, home, lifestyle, friends, contact with other family members, and so forth. The children might be leaving the nest which once again leaves room for our dreams and aspirations. The *third itch* is more of an individual and existential question where we seek to define what we want for the rest of our lives.

—*There is a difference between the first and the last "itch".*

Family Time

—The *first itch* is distinct because it is all about the need for the two partners to emotionally detach themselves from each other. We must redefine what "you" and "I" means and indeed rediscover ourselves as two individual people—after having lived a *we* life where togetherness, solidarity and the joined connections were most important. During the first couple of years we tend to be so much in love that we sometimes forget to relate actively to the world around us. As might be expected, the *first itch* is therefore about "popping the bubble". We must sort out our individual feelings and indeed understand which feelings we have. These are most likely experiences we haven't assumed responsibility for earlier on.

There are plenty of illusions—or rather delusions—about love and relationships. We genuinely believe we are fully capable of understanding the people we love. But this is not so! Reality is, that it is impossible to fully understand someone else—especially someone of the other gender. We speak such different languages, perceive the world differently and have our own distinctive approaches to life that it really is a miracle when we every now and then feel that we truly connect and are on the same wavelength. However, it is much easier getting to that beautiful feeling once we have accepted our differences. It is safe to say that it takes 15 years to get to know each other as well as we possibly can. This does require that we work really hard at it, otherwise it will take a lot longer—if it will ever happen, that is.

> *We genuinely believe we are fully capable of understanding the people we love. But this is not so! Reality is, that it is impossible to fully understanding someone else—especially someone of the other gender.*

—*Men and women interpret situations and conflicts distinctly differently. Yet "opposites attract", as the saying goes. Would those differences make it increasingly difficult to express what we really want?*

—There are many differences between women and men. In general, and remember we are talking about generalizations, women are usually more consciously aware of what they want out of a relationship. You know the classic scenario about the husband who arrives home after a day at work. The wife is preparing dinner and says: "You are not present!" to which he replies: "What do you mean, I am right here!" Then the argument begins. Had the husband listened to his wife's message he might have acknowledged and replied: "I guess you are right, I am not really here—yet!" Then the wife would have been happy. That is not the way men think because their reasoning goes like this: "If she is annoyed that I am not present then there is only one thing I can do and that is to be the way she wants me to be." In this example it means that he needs to be more present which he is not capable of. This will often lead to conflicts and many men grow tired of listening to their partner's frustrations and everything that is not right. "Why can't she just say what she wants?"

A young and perhaps inexperienced woman happily writes a long list covering everything she wants from her partner. If she does find someone who ticks all the boxes chances are that she will still not be happy. This is obviously because she now has a servant, gadget or robot-like person and not a *partner*. An older and more experienced woman would more likely say it as it is: "I want you!"

—*I know couples who take a break from their relationships in the hope that it will turn for the better when they get back together. I suspect that the break is an illusion and really the beginning of the end. What do you think?*

—I agree. During the break they realize that things are better. Many couples even enjoy a sexual relationship with each other during the break but it is different than before. Acknowledging that the relationship is about to end—or at least acknowledging that there is a risk of it ending—gives them a much greater tolerance towards each other. The problem is that they cannot live together—but they cannot figure out how to do it while they live apart. Even though it was the reason why they took the break in the first place.

Certainly, the love between two adults can cease. There is no doubt about that. If this happens there is almost no way for them to get back together again. When the love ends there is no desire left. However, the love between parent and child is different. Sure, the love might change but there is something "unconditional" about that love.

—When do we know that a relationship is about real love and not just about infatuation?

—Most of us experience a change in our hormones three to four years into the relationship. The fascination is no longer the same. Something else replaces it, namely true love. I have to stress that I don't see any value in being so rational when it comes to relationships—or having children for that matter. As humans we are highly irrational beings trying to be rational. We ask ourselves: "When can we afford children?" or "When do we have enough time for children?" It really is more important to ask: "When are we ready and mature enough to have children?" What will it be like when a new member is added to the family? We must be responsible and think rationally about things but it is important to consider the decision and its consequences on an emotional level too. Your partner might be funny and caring and the two of you might get on really well but you still have to try to figure out what he or she will be like as a parent. This might be something different all together. It is important to talk this through.

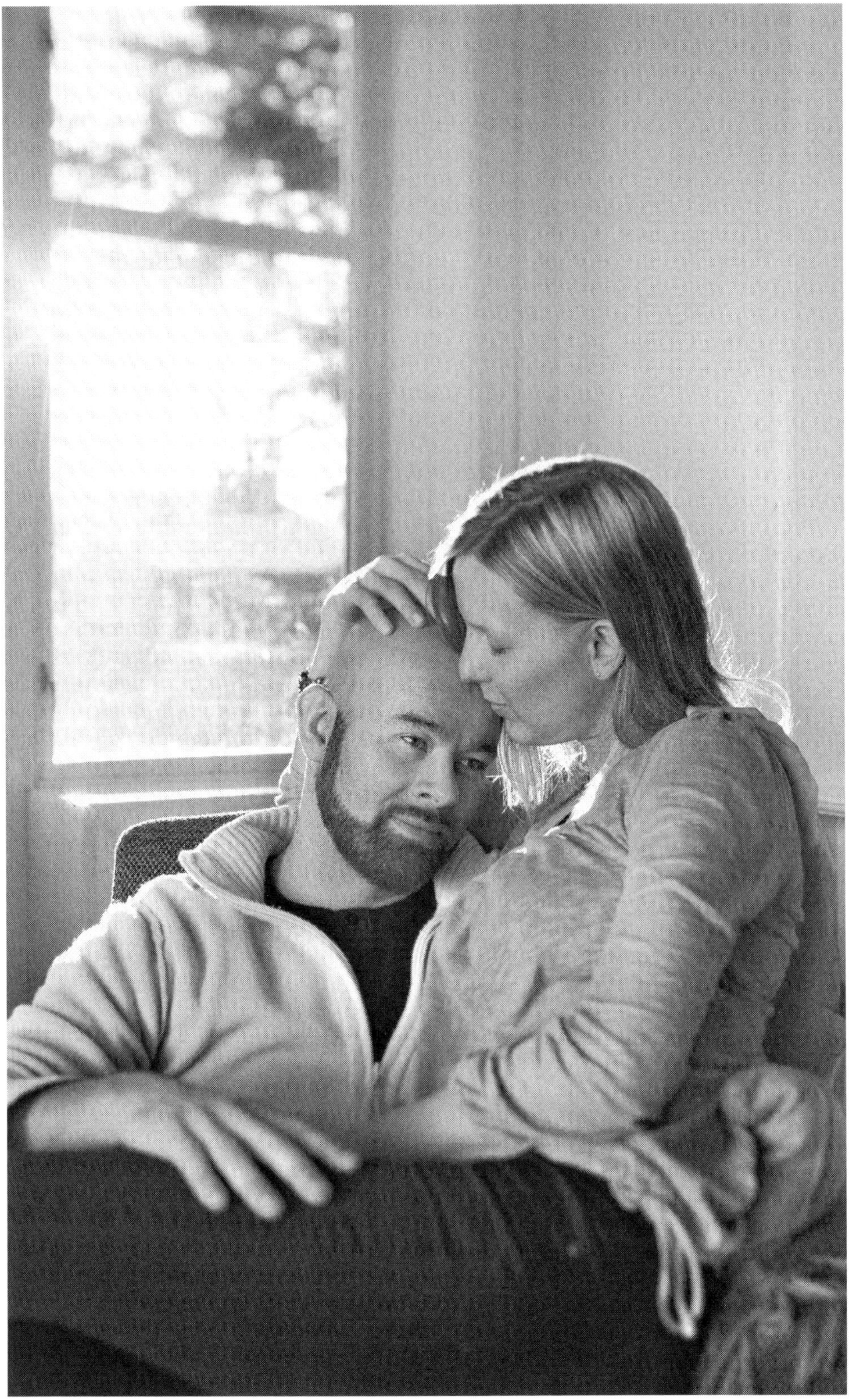

There is plenty of research that defines what it is we fall in love with. It turns out that many of the mechanisms are rather primitive. As a general, and very basic simplistic rule, women fall in love with men who have strength. Be it physical, intellectual or economic strength—men with some kind of power. The potential child that results from the relationship has to be as strong as possible. Something inside women is drawn to strength and something inside men of all ages is drawn to younger women who are fertile. We are talking about basic instincts that stem from our need to survive as a species.

During the first years of a relationship we really want to be together. It is all about love and infatuation. When I first met Suzana I liked to go shopping with her simply because she loved shopping. *Being together* was more important than what we were *doing together.* Now, she goes shopping, I find a coffee shop as quickly as possible and we agree to meet a few hours later. This is the only way for her to enjoy shopping because my aversion to it stresses her out. It is the way our love has been redefined. We must be able to let go of the idea that love means we should be able to enjoy doing everything together—including shopping and perhaps even sleeping in the same bed.

—*The parents' bedroom does set a good stage for conflicts. It might be about snoring, the room temperature, a hard or soft mattress and sexual activity.*

—Yes, there are plenty of issues to disagree about. One partner might want to sleep peacefully without being woken because of snoring. If that partner then wants to sleep in another room is not reasonable if the snorer says: "That is not my idea of living together!" You will have to modify the way you look at things. It is unreasonable to work against someone else fulfilling their personal needs. When it comes to the sexual relationship some men have to learn that women sometimes—but not always—prefer foreplay. When I talk with men I often share with them the well-known secret that the way to the bedroom goes through the living room. For many couples *good communication* is part of a fulfilling sexual relationship. Simply put, women often need more emotional contact than men do. Some men find this difficult to understand.

—*What is the key to making it work? How important is intimacy and sexuality?*

—I am challenged by the way we often talk about *eroticism* and *sexuality* in a very matter-of-fact and unemotional manner. Let us remember that any kind of sexual intercourse, which is not masturbation, has to occur between two people. And the couple can only succeed if both partners succeed. If you want your wife to do something she is not keen on it might result in her losing interest in sex all together. Then it is best not to go down that road in the first place. Why criticize your wife "until death do you part" because she doesn't have the same ideas about sexual satisfaction as you do? It is not yours or her sexuality that is at stake, it is your shared erotic universe that is at risk. This might sound more simplistic than many would hope for but at the end of the day isn't this they way it is? Criticism certainly doesn't help—I can assure you of that. Criticism only kills the sexual desire.

An expression of love must be personal. What you say to the person you love has to tell them something about what happens inside of you when the two of you are together.

—*But, many people have grown up in families and in a school system where they have been criticized and/or been praised all their lives. They have been measured and assessed on their performances and achievements. Doesn't this make it difficult for us to be able to express our feelings and have personal loving relationships?*

—What we are talking about here is *the language of love*. It is a language which we have only just started to develop. We are used to saying: "You are sexy and you are this, that and the other." It is a seductive and manipulative use of language—unsuitable for true love! It might sound wonderful to a youngster who has no self-confidence but as a 40 year old you know that it is a game without meaning.

There is a distinct difference between saying: "You are beautiful and attractive!" and "I am not sure what is happening but I feel very attracted by you!" The latter gives you the opportunity to consider the situation. There is no judgment and no option for your partner to wonder if there is a risk that he or she could also be unattractive. Instead we wonder: "What is really happening here? Why do I feel touched? Do we share something or is it simply the lower part of my body which is being affected?"

By doing this we are able to engage in a personal relationship which is not based on playing a game or playing certain tricks. I have nothing whatsoever against games or small-talk but when it comes to loving relationships we are in the process of developing a new way of expressing ourselves. Let's say your partner has just sent you a bunch of flowers. If these flowers symbolize a love that you experience while you are with him then it is beautiful. If you however, don't experience his love while you are together then the flowers will remain just flowers and an empty gesture—or a compensation for some kind of guilt perhaps?

Parents can praise their children and think that this is a way of expressing their love for them but it is really only a *symbol* of their love. An expression of love however, must by nature be personal. What you say to the person you love has to tell them something about what happens inside of you when the two of you are together. Then you use *the language of love*.

Why do misunderstandings occur in our loving relationships? Two people obviously look at the world differently. We interpret and deal with what has been said in our own personal ways. Some yell out their frustrations or cry and blame. Others internalize their sadness, they want to be alone and refuse to speak with anyone. I guess both ways of reacting say the same thing: "I want to be loved—by you!" We are just not able to express it clearly.

—When we are frustrated with our partners it is so much easier to go to war than to acknowledge the way we feel and deal with that. Why is this so?

—My wife is extremely sensitive. I might say: "Wow, it is hot today, I am sweating!" If she is not particularly warm she might start thinking that her picture of the world is wrong. When I have something to say to her which is more serious than that I must make sure she knows that it is not meant as a criticism. I now know that I must prepare her. At times, she also has to prepare me. This is what I mean when I talk about *loving behavior*.

No adults are receptive to criticism when they are frustrated. Neither are our children! They despair when they cannot work something out and in their state of frustration they are not at all able to listen to what their parents have to say. Nobody is! Nevertheless, we readily criticize each other for being like that.

Family Time

Every interaction with another person has four possible outcomes:

1. Developing the symptoms;
2. Maintaining the symptoms;
3. Reinforcing the symptoms; or
4. Healing the symptoms.

This means that the self-destructive personality traits which we carry with us from our childhoods will either be maintained or healed. Alternatively, new symptoms might develop as a consequence of the quality of the interaction. Let me give an example: A quiet man falls in love and 15 years later he has withdrawn from the relationship. This means the relationship has *reinforced the symptoms*. If he on the other hand had become more outgoing, then the relationship would have been *healing the symptoms*. If he consumed alcohol in a relaxed and reasonable manner when they met but after 15 years had become an alcoholic, then the relationship had been *developing the symptoms*.

—*It isn't always easy to be firm and take a stand against things that do not work.*

—Allow me to give you a personal example: After being a home-dad for two years I changed the focus of my work and had to spend a fair amount of my time away from home. My son's mother spent four years criticizing me for being away too much. I was unable to relate to this in any other way than to defend myself—and feel guilty. One evening something unexpected happened: We had a glass of wine and she suddenly said: "I often wonder if you miss Nikolai when you are away?" I burst into tears because this was the first time I acknowledged the great sense of sadness I felt. Until then I had not allowed myself to miss him.

We all know that criticism only makes things worse. It increases the aspects of our partners which we dislike. If you say to a man: "You work too much. You are stressed." Then he will, 99 times out of 100, start to work even more.

Many men wear blinkers and look in one direction only. When something inside us begins to protest we tell it to be quiet. From the day I allowed myself to miss my son—I worked less. This only happened because my wife met me with a genuine sense of warmth and empathy. She wondered if I missed my son and asked me about it instead of judging me and criticizing me for being away.

We all know that criticism only makes things worse. It increases those aspects of our partner's behavior which we dislike. If you say to a man: "You work too much. You are stressed." Then he will, 99 times out of 100, start to work even more. If you instead think: "Right, I have to get to know my partner better and try to work out what drives him . . ." then you will be able to sit down and say: "Quite often, I am annoyed because you work so much. But I have realized that, no matter how well I know you, I actually don't really know what drives you. Can you tell me something about what makes you do this in the first place?" If you are able to talk about things in this manner, which is far more personal, then something interesting will happen. Many men will recognize the fact that they have in fact already reached their goals a long time ago. They will also realize that they have missed out on much in the meantime.

Let us assume that your partner prioritizes work higher than anything else. Then two things can be identified:

1. He does what he has been taught, namely that he only considers himself of value to the family when he is able to

function as the breadwinner. On one level he is letting the family down by working so much but reality is that he does this precisely because he has a family. Without his family he would have taken more time off.
2. He will die early if he keeps working so hard. A little part of him dies every day. As his partner you have noticed that. How can you make it clear to him that he, to put it bluntly, is in the middle of committing suicide? Paradoxically, the reason why he works so hard in the first place will also die, namely the family.

This is challenging but it really isn't any different to a man who has a perfectionistic wife driving him crazy. She is almost obsessive because she does what she has been taught, namely that she has value to the family only when things around her are perfect. She cannot fathom that she could be worth anything if things are not perfect. Perfection is her whole identity. When that is said, we must be aware not to take away someone's identity if there is nothing to replace it with. They will lose their reason to exist.

—Do you see women as being more honest today than they were in earlier generations? Have women become better at acknowledging and expressing what they want and what they think?

—I guess it depends on the situation. When society became more affluent and the family suddenly had more money at its disposal something interesting happened within our homes. For each child to have their own room was unheard of until after the Second World War. It has become the norm that dad has a shed and/or a writing desk somewhere. It is evident that most women now also want their own space at home. It is clearly a reflection of the fact that we put a higher value on the individual. During the past 30 years ordinary women have taught us a lot, in fact much more than research has taught us. Women are voicing their opinions and talk about what they want out of relationships. Previously, nobody spoke about that—and nobody asked. The issues of pain and suffering which women have spoken about since the 1960s were unheard of before that. My father would probably have been shocked had he lived long enough to hear some of this. He made an interesting mistake: he trusted his wife. Indeed, many men do this even today but then you have to be confident that she is able to say: "Yes!" or "No!" if that is what she really means or feels. It is widely known that more women simulate orgasms than we think. Many women also accept dinner invitations simply because they are not able to say: "No thanks!"

Even though things have improved dramatically there are to this day many women who wouldn't dare to take a stand or express their own needs or opinions. In some cases this is so because the woman hasn't been taught how to. This way of being might also be so ingrained in her life that she is not able to unshackle her past. I have worked with many couples where the women says "Yes!" to everything even though she doesn't mean it. But the husband believes that they have a good relationship.

The truth always works. On a holiday not long ago we rented a little cabin. The whole family was together: my son, my two bonus sons and my partner. We were playing a card game . . . well, my partner was also playing on his iPad. This really frustrated me because nobody was able to focus. I told him a couple of times and in the end I said: "Either you play with us or your iPad!" When the children went to bed we spoke about what happened. He just wanted to do a bit of work when the others were playing. I explained to him that it felt as if he wasn't interested in the game. He didn't appreciate what I said until I told him that it meant a lot to me that we were able to play with the children. This made sense to him simply because I didn't criticize him—it came from my heart.

—We have all made mistakes in relation to our children and partners. But what happens if we don't realize until many years later, maybe the children are already teenagers. Is there still hope for the family, I mean, can we still have a genuinely good relationship?

—Sure. All you have to do is stop doing what you have been doing and do something different.

Responsibility is the only medication that works against *guilt*. Think things through and talk about them with you partner if you have one and go to your child and say: "Listen, we have done the wrong things for the first 12 years of your life. We thought that it was our duty to make sure you didn't get frustrated. We were wrong! We will stop doing it if we are able to. We are absolutely certain that you will manage but we will most likely continue making the same mistake—at least until we get used to the new way."

Obviously, there are some kinds of guilt for which there is no medicine. If abuse has happened or violence is involved then the guilt will last for the rest of our lives. One of the aspects that differentiates us from animals is the fact that we can feel guilt when we do something wrong. This is good but I don't accept long drawn-out feelings of guilt. It is only an excuse for being passive and for allowing yourself to worry. One could say that holding on to guilt is like a rocking chair: You can keep rocking but you will never get anywhere.

—*Many of us find it difficult to remember actual stories from our childhoods. It is easier to remember the feeling of anxiety, happiness, a smell, a reaction . . . !*

—The more traumatic a childhood has been the less we remember. The brain is very clever that way. We probably wouldn't have been able to survive as a species if we didn't have the ability to *repress*. Some people might have had an absolutely terrible childhood but remember it as a happy time all the same. We have an incredible ability to cooperate and adjust. It actually makes sense if it turns out that relationship number two, three or four will deal with some of those things. At that stage we might be mature enough to approach the issues. Many will experience a "reality check" when they enter a relationship that seems 100% perfect. You are happy because you have married the right one, yet one month later you are depressed. I have met many couples who are very confused and frustrated when this happens. More often than not, the husband is confused and I have to tell him that he ought to take it as a compliment. His wife has finally found a space where she is comfortable enough to let go of her pain. "But what should I do?" he asks. The answer is that he should not do anything at all. He just needs to make sure that she is safe, give her a hug and then she has to be allowed to cry. He doesn't need to worry about her. It is an expression of love when we allow others to be the way they are.

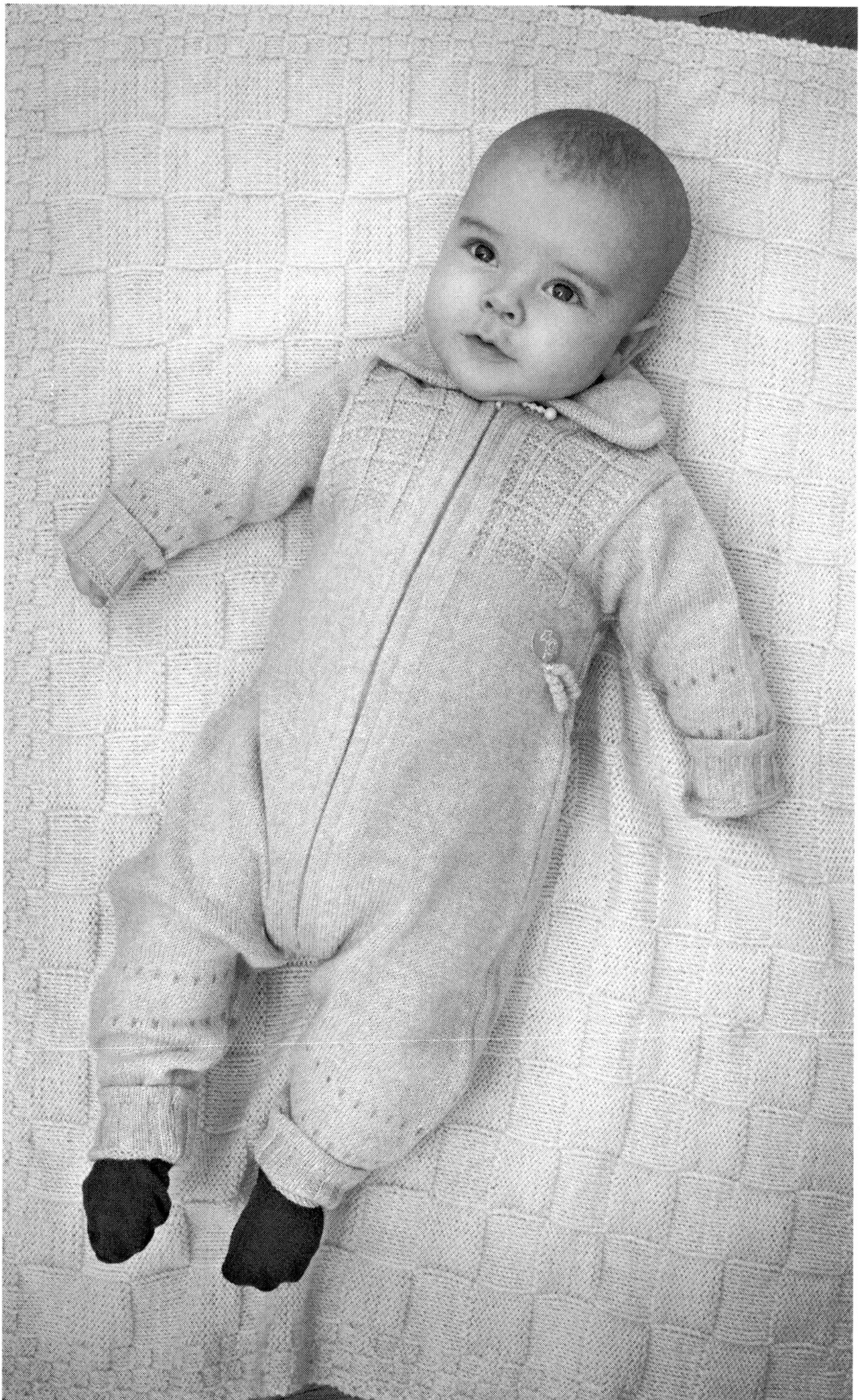

THE BABY'S ROOM
– Emotions and closeness

It is an upheaval of serious proportions to welcome a baby into a family. It changes the love nest and every other aspect of the intimacy between two people who love each other. The baby might take up a lot of space—sometimes perhaps too much! The father might find himself sidelined. The mother might be so absorbed that she is unable to do and talk about anything else other than the baby.

Every dream you might have as a couple could burst if you completely give in to parenting and forget or fail to attend to the relationship with your partner. It is easy to forget. For the time being it is the baby who is the main focus.

MONICA:
—I often wonder how a pregnant mother's lifestyle influences the unborn baby. Is the baby affected by what the mother eats and by her physical and emotional well-being?

JESPER:

—The child will, without doubt, be healthier when the mother is healthy and sticks to the set guidelines about what she should and should not eat and drink.

That said, there is no research which indicates that the unborn child has sensorial experiences similar to its mother when it comes to food, physical and emotional health. However, recent studies do show that the child's sense of taste is influenced by what the mother eats during pregnancy.

It is also reasonable to assume that the mother's way of dealing with her pregnancy influences the child's psyche. Most notably whether or not the child feels, and indeed is, wanted.

For more than 15 years I worked with single mothers from lower social economic groups. They would often, quite openly, say to me that their newborn child was really meant to have been "just a stain on the sheet". The unborn baby's capacity to sense or be influenced by the mother's emotions is what we have defined as *tuning-in*. It is a capacity that the baby develops subconsciously and enables the baby to *tune-in* to the mother's emotions and state of mind. It is safe to say that many mothers have intuitively sensed this and that the *tuning-in* between mother and baby has always happened. We just haven't been able to define it more accurately until recently. I am confident that the capacity for *tuning-in* is heredity and that baby and mother develop this as early as during the final trimester of pregnancy. In other words; *tuning-in* is a unique capacity that a baby inherently develops in unison with the mother while she is pregnant. This means that the baby is able to experience and share the mother's emotions.

For the father to familiarize himself with his unborn baby requires a highly sensitive emotional capacity. This is indeed difficult—even once the baby is newborn. Mothers have a kind of radar which most fathers do not develop. For years I have been saying to mothers: "Take a holiday for about a week when your baby is around 12 months old." This gives the father a unique opportunity to be alone with your baby 24/7. From the time when my son was six months until he turned two years I was at home all day while my wife studied. The responsibility was mine—and mine alone. I certainly wasn't the baby's nanny or babysitter, I was the baby's father. I believe that any mother ought to let go and give the father this opportunity. It will, in fact, be good for her too. She will ultimately get a true parenting partner instead of a little relief now and then. All this is also a real benefit to the baby.

When a woman gives birth she will experience one of love's best kept secrets. She will experience that the love she receives from the baby only comes second to the love she is able to give. This might start during pregnancy or straight after the birth. She will most certainly feel that love to its fullest when she breast-feeds (if she is able to). This is not an experience available to men. Quite a number of men believe that receiving is better than giving. Consequently, some fathers become frustrated when their partners no longer want to or simply aren't able to give them all they need. She might stop taking a sincere interest in his life. Perhaps she is also, for the time being, not too passionate about their love life.

> *When a woman gives birth she will experience one of love's best kept secrets. She will experience that the love she receives from the baby only comes second to the love she is able to give.*

The father will be rewarded beyond expectation if he is able to get involved right from the beginning. He ought to do this primarily for his own sake. It is good for the baby too but it is wrong to get involved only for the baby's sake. In a number of articles and books, high-powered executives have noted that they were fortunate to be able to take three to six months paternity leave. This taught them more than any executive seminars ever could. It is about learning to deal with personal relationships, closeness, planning and indeed learning to multi-task. The father ought to allow himself this opportunity. Most fathers who take this time also experience a level of happiness they cannot attain anywhere else. He will be rewarded for giving and sharing of his love, and for going through the personal development, which inevitably comes from allowing a baby to slip inside his life. First he must honestly answer this question, though: "Do I really want to do it or would I rather do something else?" When he knows the answer he must share it with his partner in a way that is neither indecisive nor threatening. She must willingly agree that it is the right answer. Once he has made up his mind it is easier to change direction later on. If he doesn't make a firm decision and ends up walking around feeling uncomfortable everything will be more complicated.

—When the mother lets go and hands over some responsibility to the father she will also learn to trust him?

—Certainly! Before the mother takes her break when the baby is around 12 months old I actually tell her that she is not allowed to phone home during the break. She has to go away and she has to let go. Hand over, trust and allow him to take full responsibility. It is alright for him to phone her, but she is not allowed to check in. If that happens the father will be *remote-controlled.*

When I was at home with our son we lived in a house with other families. As I took him out I had to go through the common room. I would meet other mothers who gladly shared with me their opinions about what I was doing. And they were never short of "good" advice. I quickly learned to speak up and to show them that I wanted to do things my way. I literally experienced a degree of "mother chauvinism"—the mothers were convinced that they were right and that fathers weren't good enough.

In some European cultures it is custom that the baby spends all its time with the mother during the first three to four years. Only then will the father get involved. From infant research we know that a baby benefits considerably from an equally strong connection with both mother and father. Psychology used to tell us that a baby prefers to be with his or her mother. Today we know better. We know this is not right. Yet, if the father considers himself simply as a nanny or babysitter then the baby will naturally resist forming a close bonding with him. Only around 10% of the post-war generation children had a connection with the father during their first 12 months. Today we are moving closer to 50%. It makes an enormous difference to the baby's future. During the past couple of years fathers have started defining a new role for themselves, which is not merely based on a poor imitation of the mother's role. In many Northern European cities you will find an increasing amount of fathers with their babies at the libraries and in coffee shops.

—In other words; society has become a better place for fathers. But many mothers still see it as a given that the baby and child have more extended contact with her than with the father.

—Reality is that most mothers have most of the contact. In the old days it was very common that the father hardly ever spent time with the baby. A few decades ago the upper classes would hire a nanny, au pair or a governess. As a consequence both parents were, in truth, absent. The nanny would change the baby, feed it, bathe it, look after it when it was sick and put it to bed. The parents would only see the baby when it was clean and healthy or asleep—when it was easy to deal with.

Family Time

This brought about some awful consequences. The crucially important contact and bond between parents and children, which has to be established during the first four years, simply didn't develop. When there is not enough contact between parents and children they will grow up being restless, unsettled and without knowing their roots. Some children resign themselves and give up. Others might become very quiet and introverted.

—Can we go back to the infant for a moment? Some babies scream the house down if they are nursed by others than the parents—some babies don't even want to be nursed by the father.

—Does the baby want to be with the mother because the baby likes her comfort? Allow me to challenge you: Is it in some cases possible that the nursing also provides the mother some comfort? This scenario is possible and the only one who really knows the answer is the mother.

—Some children instantly trust and feel comfortable with other people while others continue to feel uncomfortable.

—My observations tell me that we can divide children into two groups—generally speaking. Those who immediately develop a good relationship with adults, and those who keep some distance until they feel that they can trust the adults. The people close to the baby might experience that a four or five months old baby cannot handle close contact for much more than 30 seconds. If you ignore this, or even worse, take it personally, then the baby will scream and cry, and feel very uncomfortable indeed. Perhaps the baby only needs 10 to 15 seconds rest before it is ready to try again.

—My girlfriend had a baby who just wouldn't stop screaming. She thought the issue was colic but that turned out not to be the case.

What are you supposed to do when a baby just cannot stop screaming even though it is perfectly healthy?

—You must take the baby seriously. Create as much peace and calm as you are able to, and make sure the baby feels safe. Then you simply have to wait until the screaming stops. If you ask people who claim to have supernatural abilities they will tell you that "a child chooses its parents". I don't know if this is true but it is evident that every baby is born with some patterns of reaction which are not due to the parents' characteristics or birth experiences. Nevertheless, the parents will learn a lot from the challenges that arise when they have close contact with their newborn baby.

When my son was six months old he was admitted to hospital. He had a cyst on his neck and the doctors examined him from top to toe. Five long and worrying days later they were able to tell me that it was a benign cyst. Afterwards I would still worry. I should probably have tried to come to terms with my reactions differently. For months I was very protective and would always worry. Fortunately, I learned that it was an emotional fear and not a rational fear. He had his own bedroom early on and we soon found a way for all of us to feel comfortable about it. Nevertheless, as a new parent you hit the ground running. You have to learn everything—not just read about it but experience it!

—*I guess it is challenging for parents to sleep with a baby in the room. Does a baby really need to sleep in there and when is the baby ready to "move out"?*

—I honestly believe that there are no set answers to this. Historically speaking, children have never had their own rooms. That only started some time after the Second World War simply because families had more money and more space. My grandson only slept in his parents'

Family Time

room while he was breast-feeding. When he has a sleep-over at our place he also prefers his own room.

While breast-feeding it is probably most practical to let the baby sleep in the same room as the mother. But, if the parents agree, then it is also perfectly alright to let the baby have his/her own room. However, if the parents feel guilty about "kicking" the baby out and suspect that it cries all night because it is unhappy or lonely then they might want to reconsider. If letting the baby sleep in the parents' room makes them happy I am absolutely certain that the baby will feel happier too.

It is important that the parents think the issues through and are clear with each other. If they don't agree they might be better off not making decisions straight away. It is not possible to live in a loving relationship if difficulties are allocated into your *problems* and my *problems*. The challenges and problems must be *ours*. In case parents disagree they ought to wait changing things until they are both ready. If the mother wishes to wait letting the baby "move out" then the father also has to wait until she is ready—and the other way around. One parent simply has to wait for the other.

> *It is not possible to live in a loving relationship if difficulties are allocated into your problems and my problems. The challenges and problems must be ours.*

—Many parents feel that they must succeed in everything they do with their children. Say, parents are restless and insecure, and they worry about not being able to get the children to sleep then there is very little change the baby will fall asleep without a lot of stress and fuss?

—Some parents are not aware of this but around 40% of all children find it difficult to fall asleep. It has always been like that and it is like that all over the world regardless of culture and traditions. These days everything surrounding our children is very important and we take things very seriously—almost too seriously. Perhaps we need to look at things from a different perspective. On a busy day some parents might not be able to spend more than 30 to 45 minutes of quiet time with their children, maybe this is before bedtime. That is when they can get to know each other and they can do wonderful things together. Chat, read, sing or whatever. In some families, this time becomes rather stressful because so much "has" to be done. Evening time should really be spent following a few simple routines and calming the child. I have experienced parents who made the most of this opportunity and didn't get stressed about making the child go to bed—as you will have guessed, the child went to sleep without any dramas.

There are many different techniques and strategies you can try if you want children to go to sleep. I am not a great supporter of what is known as *controlled crying*. The technique where you let the baby cry for a while before you return to give some comfort. Then you let the child cry for longer and longer periods. It is obviously fine for parents to try this technique. However, if it doesn't work after four days I think they must stop. It really is child abuse. This method started in England and the aim was to help the baby *self-soothe*. The baby is meant to learn to soothe and calm itself during very difficult situations. One of the most difficult situations for a baby is to calm down to such a degree that it is able to fall asleep. A researcher from South Africa hypothesizes that there is a correlation between *controlled crying* and the abuse of alcohol, drugs and antidepressants later on. He argues that when an eight to ten month old infant learns that pain and frustration is something it cannot share with others it will have learned a lesson for life. In adult life the person will find it almost impossible to ask parents or friends for help if something is wrong precisely because it was forced to deal with pain on his/her own as a baby.

I think it might be more useful if the parents ask themselves how they manage in similar situations. All you need to do is to lie down on the bed with your partner when he or she is nervous or restless. You will realize how difficult it is to fall asleep. The child will feel exactly the same way when this kind of emotional noise is present and comes from inside of you.

It is, as we know, impossible to be happy, content and full of energy all day and every day. Your child needs to learn and live with that. You can say: "Darling, I am really frustrated and not feeling well tonight. Can you do me a big favor and go to sleep by yourself?" Most likely they will say: "Yes, that's fine with me!" Children really do want to please their parents but the parents have to teach them. Remember, children don't learn like students do. They learn like researchers so they need to find the solutions themselves. When we as parents try all kinds of techniques to make our children fall asleep they will never be able to explore and find their own ways.

—Does this mean that a child who falls sleeps easily is more harmonious?

—Maybe, but there are many reasons why children don't fall asleep easily. Perhaps they have experienced something uncomfortable during the day? Adults cannot fall asleep on cue either. Ironically—and regrettably, when children don't sleep parents often won't get enough sleep either. That is why it is so important for parents to make sure they get some sleep while their child actually sleeps. Otherwise you will yourself become sleep deprived.

—How about "adult time"? How do you tell the child that you also need space and time to yourselves as a couple?

—You certainly need that. But if you tell your child this and use the wrong sort of expression then it will feel like a burden. Perhaps you could try to say: "I want to spend a couple of hours in peace and quiet with you father. I would like you to spend some time in your room. Call me if you need any help, then I will be there."

—I was so fortunate that my son hardly ever cried when he went to bed. He dozed off with his teddy listening to some music. It took him about 20 minutes to fall asleep.

—The reason why you had no problems with your son's sleep is not because he is unique in any way. He is just used to a mother with authority. You don't deal with compromises and you rarely give in. You set the agenda and to a large extent decide what happens. This is an authority your son is used to. When I finally worked out how to use my authority I found it easier to get on with children.

Allow me to share a funny experience: We live on the 3rd floor. When my grandson, Alex was 15 months old he wanted to play in the hallway with my wife. Suddenly he wanted to crawl down the fire escape and she said: "Well, we can do that, but I have to put my shoes on first." She said this in a way many women do, apologetically. Children pick up on this and they get frustrated. His reaction was to become irritated and impatient. He made it clear that he thought he had to wait for too long. The following week I said: "Alex, I would like to go down the fire escape with you but first I have to put my shoes on." I put my shoes on and there were no problems. The situation repeated itself in the afternoon. For some reason, I was hoping he didn't want to go down the fire escape again so I hadn't put my shoes on. Nevertheless, he wanted to go down and I said: "No!" It didn't take him long to find my shoes because he wanted to go.

—*He knew what had to happen before he could get what he wanted.*

—Exactly! That is simply because I had a firm voice which clearly sent the message: that's the way things are going to happen. When a spoken message is delivered with an apologizing expression it becomes a message of uncertainty.

—*Clear and specific messages create security and confidence?*

—If I say: "Alex, I need to cook dinner now, you will need to play on your own!" I might have a crying child—but that will last for all of 15 seconds. After that he will play on his own. If my wife wants the same thing it sounds more like: "I am very sorry, but . . ." Then Alex will be frustrated because he doesn't know what to do or how to deal with it. But he does know how to deal with a message that is delivered with confidence and is specific.

Development of a child's *personal authority* is not something that is encouraged at home, in child care centers or at school. The main focus of these institutions is really to make children adjust and fit in. The sooner and the more obedient children adjust to the system—the better they are liked and the better results they will be able to achieve. When they leave the institution, reality hits. If they only master the ability to adjust they won't go far. Job prospects will be limited because interesting jobs are for people who show initiative, take responsibility and have an opinion. These jobs are not for people who always need to ask how to do things. It is *creativity* that our societies and economies needs. These days there is very little need for soldiers and production line workers. Perhaps the school system produces children for an industrial society—one which really doesn't exist any longer.

Some parents fear to demonstrate authority because they don't want to be seen as authoritarian. Nonetheless, it is absolutely possible to develop ones personal authority without being authoritarian, which is necessary for meaningful personal relationships.

—*Do some people confuse the terms being an* authority *with being* authoritarian?

—This is true. Someone who commands authority is one who has the ability to make an impact and influence others through their recognized knowledge. Whereas, an authoritarian person is one who shows lack of concern for the wishes of others. After years of fighting for freedom and against authoritarian systems some parents fear to demonstrate authority because they don't want to be seen as authoritarian. Nonetheless, it is absolutely possible to develop ones personal authority without being authoritarian. This is, in fact, necessary for meaningful personal relationships.

Not understanding these distinctions is part of what makes life difficult for parents as well as teachers. It is also what causes many unnecessary and avoidable problems between adults, children and youth.

I have babysat plenty of children throughout the years. I remember a girl who just didn't want to sleep on her own. We had a wonderful evening, baked a cake and made a little bracelet. Nevertheless, this girl refused to sleep on her own. I had to lie down next to her until she fell asleep. That was what her mother or father did every night. It wasn't difficult to see who was the boss in their home.

—*You have written much about our children being competent. What kind of abilities are they born with?*

—The theories of *developmental psychology* tried to teach me that children are not competent and that it takes them around 18 years before they turn into decent grown-up adults. I have personally experienced something different, namely that a baby is born with plenty of competencies which are similar to those of an adult. They are born with empathy, social needs, initiative, the ability to take responsibility for themselves in a number of areas as well as a knowledge of their own limits. When that is said, we must remember that although children are competent this doesn't mean that they are able to do everything. They cannot take responsibility—or even part of the responsibility—for the relationships with their parents and other adults. Neither can they look after themselves sufficiently until the age of nine or ten.

—*Perhaps parents should try to see their children's abilities and inspire them to develop these in the best possible way.*

—When we are aware of children's competencies, and value these, they will develop naturally. If children are seen and listened to they grow and become more nuanced human beings. If, on the other hand, their competencies are not acknowledged they will become either extremely difficult or very helpless. The most important thing to remember is that children's reactions are always meaningful. You can safely trust their responses. You will then have to work out what kind of guidance they need. Children are born with plenty of wisdom but without experiences. They have a need for experienced guides.

When they are still babies we should ideally be able to distinguish between seven or eight different cries; those that mean frustration, pain, danger, etc. When parents are unable to tell the difference they become confused as soon as the child makes a sound—especially around bedtime. No one should be left alone with their unhappiness. Particularly not babies!

Children are born with plenty of wisdom but without experiences.

—If the baby isn't tired when put down, should we just leave them crying?

—Sure. It is very interesting that most parents stop searching for answers as soon as their children learn to speak—at the same time this is frightening. The first 16 to 18 months we try to tune into all the signals they send. Which sounds mean: "I'm hungry!" or "I'm tired" and so forth. As soon as the child begins to speak things change. We think we know the child well enough and don't need to get to know them any better. We are no longer interested in seeing them grow, search and explore the world. Instead we give them the answers to what is right and wrong. Just because children develop an oral language doesn't mean we know who they are. Every day they absorb and learn thousands of new things. The child you pick-up from childcare in the afternoon is not the same one you dropped off in the morning.

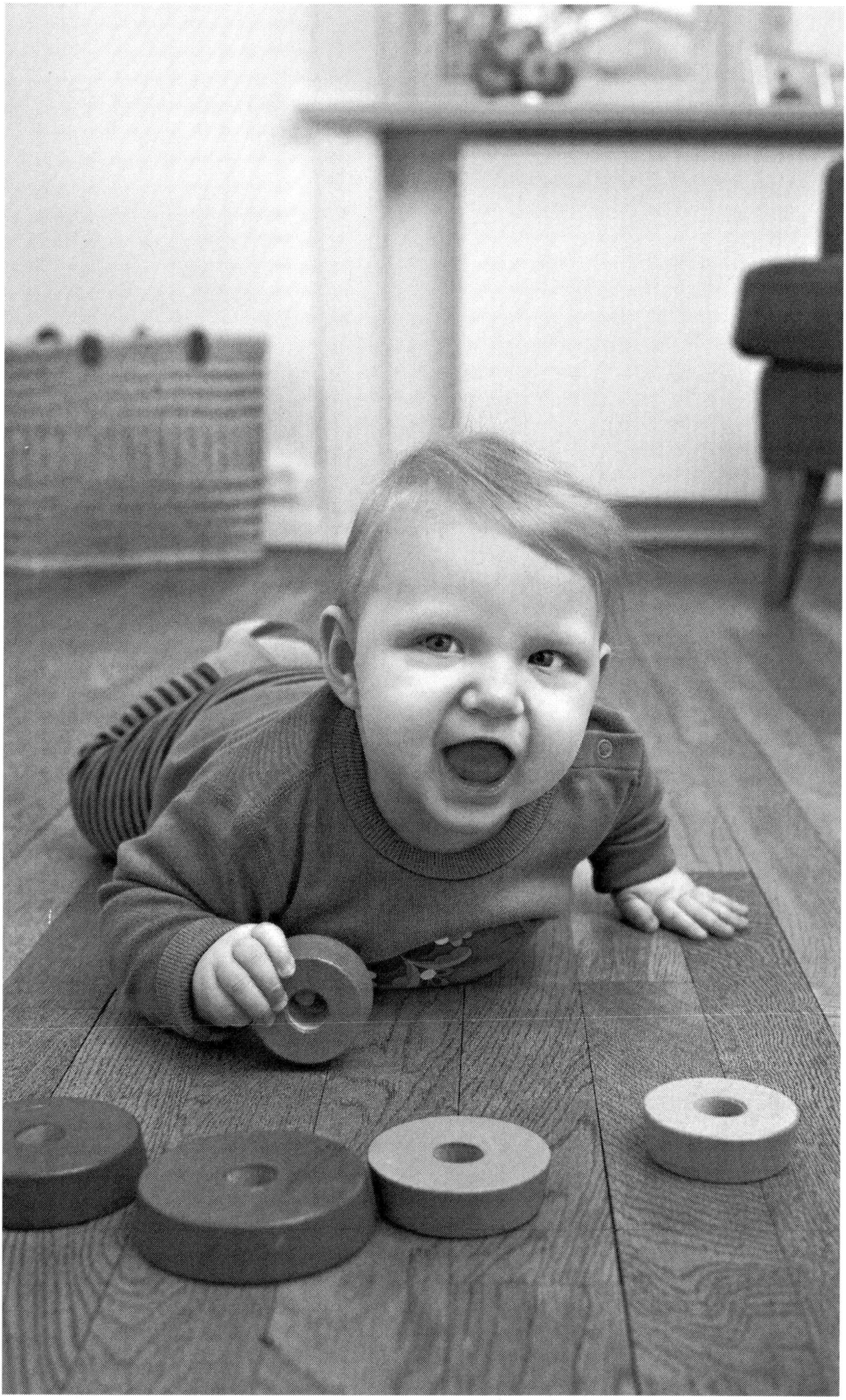

The notion that we as parents know what is best for our children is nonsense. It is much better to continue being curious and engaged. Study the child's body language, tone of voice, looks and so forth. Most parents forget this and focus completely on *raising* their children.

—*At what age does the child begin to take personal responsibility?*

—The very moment they are born! Let me share with you the findings of a research project which was conducted in 1975. The Swiss doctor, Remo Largo worked with all the babies (and their parents) who were born that year in one hospital. One half of the parents let the children take responsibility for their own appetite. They were only fed when they indicated to the mothers that they were hungry, and it was considered that they had enough when they pulled away from the breast. For the other half it was up to the mothers to control this. The children were then observed and followed for years. It became clear that those who were allowed to take responsibility for themselves were better off on every account. They had no major behavioral problems, no psycho-social problems, no obesity and no anorexia.

—*With that in mind, do you think it should be up to the child when it wants to eat?*

—What we put into our mouths and when we do it ought to be the very first of our human rights.

Throughout my childhood it was common practice to use "baby language" when speaking with children. Adults thought they had to "dumb down". It was actually seen as a positive and pedagogically correct way of interacting. In doing so, adults became actors because it wasn't genuine. The tone of voice used can send completely different messages compared to the actual words spoken. We need to practice being genuine and communicate on a personal level with children and adults alike. That will only improve the communication – and the relationship.

—Some children will be chatterboxes when they start to speak. Meanwhile, other parents begin to wonder what is wrong with their children if they aren't speaking when they turn two or three years of age. These differences cause some kind of concern and parents often blame themselves.

—The fact is however, that some children develop their speech later than others but then they have a larger passive vocabulary. Once they start speaking they will pick it up really quickly. It might depend on how much the parents speak with them and if they speak properly—without using *baby language*. The more stories we read to children the sooner and better they develop their language. In the everyday interactions it is important to use your own language—even if the child doesn't understand every single word. This is the way they learn. The first couple of weeks it really isn't so important what we say, what is important is the sound of your voice.

A message contains two things: The actual words and the tone of voice. Many parents feel frustrated when their children don't listen. This is often because they don't use their own language – instead they use a "child-friendly" language.

A message contains two things: The actual words and the tone of voice. Many parents feel frustrated when their children don't listen. This is often because they don't use their own language – instead they try to use a "child-friendly" language. We don't need to worry about the fact that children don't understand some of the words we use. They get the message anyway. They understand that things are serious when someone gets angry. It is not a good idea trying to be pedagogical about it. This horrible and supposedly "child-friendly" way of speaking to children was invented sometime in the 1960s. It is useless simply because it really doesn't have any substance. The thought was to consider the child but when the words and the tone of voice are different there is confusion and children don't learn to master their own language properly.

In some schools the old school books were replaced by comic books because it was thought that the comics books were at a better level for children. It cannot come as a surprise if there is a decline in children's general knowledge and abilities. They get used to a simple and primitive language. When they read some of the classics they might have to struggle to understand but they will certainly develop a richer and more nuanced language.

If your partner says: "I love you!" you can easily sense if it a routine statement or if it indeed comes from the heart. Children sense that too. They know when you speak from the heart. It is important that you send the whole and honest message otherwise it is not going to work. It is really important the whole message is communicated otherwise it doesn't have any impact. When parents complain that their children do not listen it is often because their words lack "music". The message doesn't contain their own words, thoughts and emotions. It is probably not a coincidence that many Indigenous peoples sing when they experience a crisis. They express both the words and the music.

> *If your partner says: "I love you!" you can easily sense if it a routine statement or if it indeed comes from the heart. Children sense that too. They know when you speak from the heart.*

—What you are saying is challenging and requires some kind of self-realization. It might be difficult knowing what frame of mind or mood you are in and it does require that you know yourself pretty well.

—I honestly don't think it is that demanding or difficult. Remember, parents who speak to their children in a fake *baby language* are in fact also able to speak to their partners, colleagues, friends and family in a perfectly normal language. For some reason people think the child needs an amputated language. When you say this to your child: "Now, your mother is going to get really angry!" then you are speaking as if you are your own psychologist. You will be *describing* yourself instead of *expressing* yourself. The difficult part is clearly to express what you feel. Top musicians do not just learn the notes because notes are not music. Musicians have to give so much of themselves before it is worth listening to.

One of the many presents children give parents is an invitation to learn this language. Otherwise, the relationship isn't going to work. From day one, children express themselves with all of their body but very often all they get is a readymade answer. It is absurd when parents everywhere talk about themselves in third person: "Dad thinks it is time for bed." Children don't get it. Instead they look at the dad with a blank face. "Is there a dad here who I can't see?" or "Is he talking about his own dad?" 90% of what we do with our children we ought to test on adults. If it doesn't work with other adults it isn't going to work on children either. I can't say to my wife: "Your husband doesn't feel like buying you perfume." When parents speak to children like that they believe they are being kind. In actual fact, they do the opposite. They hide between words and role-playing. That is when their children start testing boundaries to find out who their parents are, what they feel and what really is behind the roles they play.

I can't help but make some associations to the parents' relationship. Some parents are loving towards each other whilst others live in a kind of *facade relationship* where they simply act. The odd thing is that the very same mother who often speaks to her child in baby language will turn around to her husband and complain to him about not being present. The mother knows that love requires a language with substance, personality and feelings. Nevertheless, she speaks to her child in *baby language*. As a result, the child doesn't like listening to her let alone respond to what she says. Even the most well educated parents don't understand why their children stop communicating. When that happens it is about time to stop wondering what is wrong with the child and start focusing on how things are actually said to them. Children must learn to express themselves and not just learn to chat.

We all know people who speak very eloquently but they don't say much. Most of it is a selection of obvious statements and superficial chatting. This might work well in social settings, at work or in politics but intimate relationships require more than that—the conversation has to be genuine. The good thing is that parents will see a very rapid improvement as soon as they start using their personal language, and then they won't stop because it works so well and is highly rewarding.

—*What do you really mean by "personal language"?*

—It is the core of what we are all about. When we are personal we say: "I want this and I don't want that!" and "I like this and I don't like that!" when we speak about ourselves, our feelings, our values, our boundaries and so forth. We need to use a personal language when we wish to define our personal integrity. Other people are able to find out who we are when we use personal language. This means we will be able to relate to each other with sincerity and authenticity.

> *We need to use a personal language when we wish to define our personal integrity. Other people are able to find out who we are when we use personal language. This means we will be able to relate to each other with sincerity and authenticity.*

—Could you give me some examples? I mean, how can parents use their personal language when speaking with each other and their children?

—It is a good idea to use exactly the same kind of language when speaking with a newborn as you would with an adult—and your partner for that matter. Let me give you an example: A woman made an appointment to see me. She brought her four months old baby. Her best friend had lost her 18 months old baby due to heart failure. The woman who saw me was also grieving as she was very sorry about what had happened. While I spoke with her she started breast-feeding. This went well until the mother started to cry. The baby let go and looked at her with a sad and worried face. "What am I supposed to do?" she asked me. I replied: "You should tell your baby exactly the same as you told me before." She did and the baby smiled, looked comfortable and started sucking again. Babies do not intellectually understand what we say to them (as far as we know) but they do understand the tone of voice and the atmosphere of what is being said. As soon as the baby was given an explanation she calmed down even though she didn't understand the words. It is crucially important that we use our own personal language and we don't try to modify it when we speak with children.

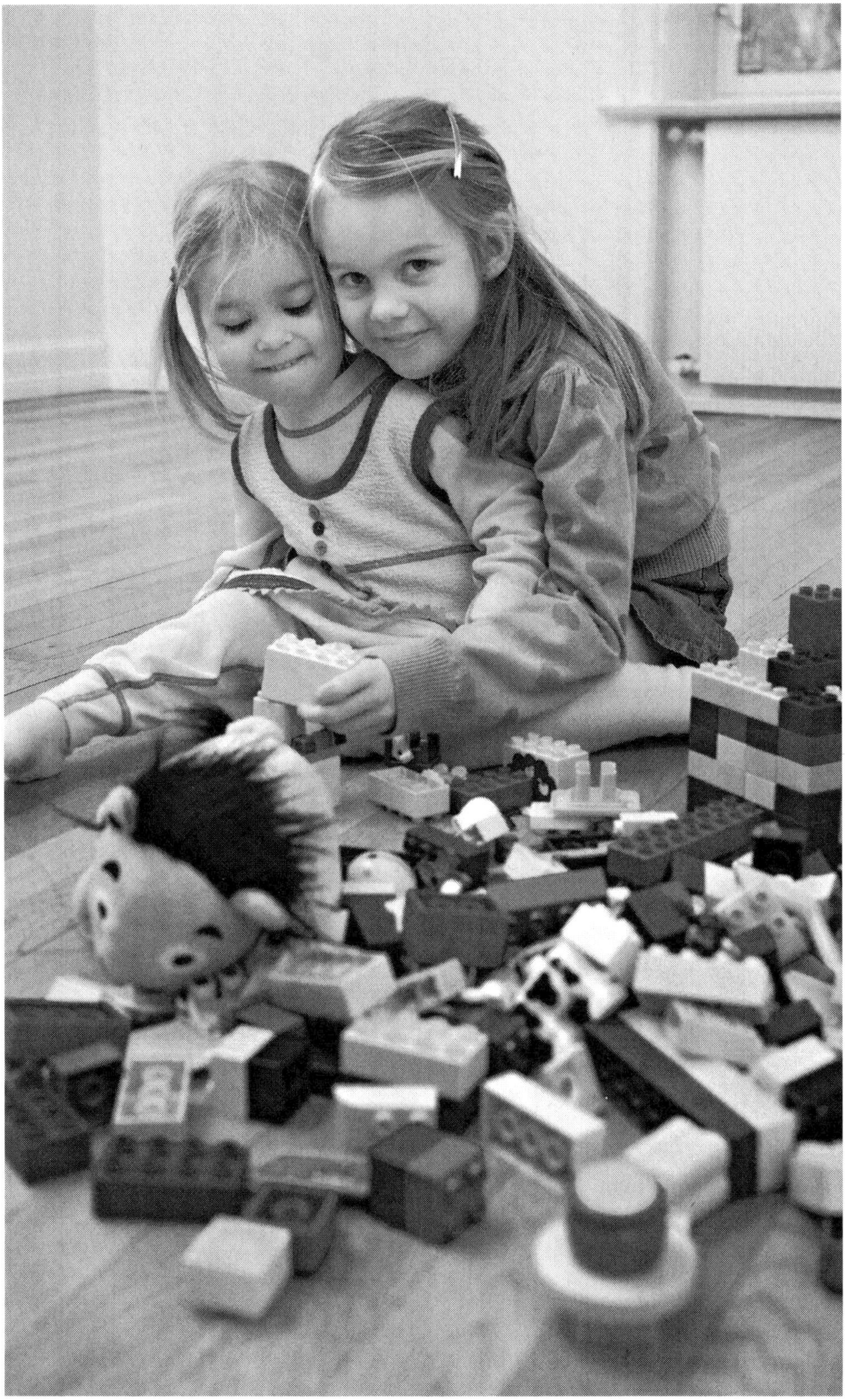

THE CHILD'S ROOM
– Play and independence

What do you remember from your childhood? I remember a few emotional experiences but the physical experiences are the ones I remember most clearly. I remember smells, such as the smell of the laundry in our beach house. It was the laundry powder, I think. When I smell something similar today I am brought right back to that very same beach house. I also remember I was furious one Sunday when I was five years old. I did not want to visit my aunt, Lynn. I felt angry—but I also remember that I felt very uneasy about the anger. I wanted to stop being angry but I couldn't.

MONICA:
—The first time young children try to break away from their parents is when they reach the so-called "Terrible Twos", "Trouble Twos", "The Phase of Defiance", "The Troublemaker Twos" or however we describe them. Why do children get angry and become frustrated during those years?

JESPER:
—It is very unfortunate that psychologists, doctors, nurses, carers and others use the term *terrible twos*—they should know better. If a mother wants to put a t-shirt on her two year old son but he wants to do it himself she might get annoyed and say: "You can't do it yet, let me!" Ultimately, we project our own anger onto our children and we will soon claim that they are the ones who are angry. We then attach a label to this and similar events. We teach our children a certain way of being, namely our way!

The boy mentioned above will not have learned how to dress himself. All he learns is *helplessness*. We make them helpless by continually telling them that we as adults can do things better. Children don't learn by being taught—they learn by exploring and experimenting. It is not a surprise that they become frustrated when we lecture to them. If parents label their frustration as *anger* they will naturally start doing the same, namely meeting anger with anger.

> *I refer to the so-called "terrible twos" (or whatever we call them) as the "independent years". I believe that we as parents are able to approach those years with a sense of relief. Instead of expecting problems we should think: "Finally, they are gaining some independence."*

I refer to the so-called *terrible twos* (or whatever we call them) as the *independent years*. I believe that we as parents are able to approach those years with a sense of relief. Instead of expecting problems we should think: "Finally, they are gaining some independence." In terms of their development they certainly become more independent because they are able to do more things by themselves as opposed to having everything done for them. From a pedagogical point of view children are very sophisticated. They continually challenge themselves with tasks that are a little bit too difficult. If they want to dress themselves or tie shoelaces before they are able to, then let them try—even if you know it is going to go horribly wrong. Children learn from trying. They explore theories and hypotheses, and will learn just as much when they fail as when they succeed. They don't learn like school students do. Students are fed knowledge but young children experiment. They believe they can tie the shoelaces and try. They might not succeed so they try again and again and . . . one day they get it right. That's why it is a good idea to let them try and allow them to persevere without doing it for them.

> *If this behavior and this important phase in their lives are attached a negative label then we have made a problem out of something that is really a gift. The process of trying, improving, developing and evolving is completely human.*

If this behavior and this important phase in their lives are attached a negative label then we have made a problem out of something that is really a gift. The process of trying, improving, developing and evolving is completely human. When parents worry about this then they will be in for a difficult time. Not because of the nature of the child but because it has become part of the parents' expectations which therefore become part of the child's behavior.

Parents' attitudes when their children are two or three years old have an important influence on what will happen during puberty. Puberty is the second opportunity they have for finding themselves. If parents have fought against their children during the *independent years* then they can look forward to a similar resistance when they reach puberty. These parents will be in for some very serious power struggles. By looking back at your children's lives and their way of learning during the *independent years* you are able to prepare for some of what you can expect during their teenage years.

—I would like to talk more about puberty later but while we are on this issue: does it mean that parents have a second chance?

—That's right! Let me make it very clear: it is never too late for parents to change their approach, behavior and attitude, and do things differently. During the *independent years* children are presented with their first opportunity to take some big steps—or giant leaps—in terms of developing their self-confidence and self-worth. They learn about their potential—and their limitations. They learn to master different skills and that is all part of developing their self-confidence. You should offer them your support as they must learn the value of asking for help—and feel that this is perfectly fine. When they need help it is obviously not because they are silly but it must be up to them whether or not they need help. Helping without being asked is not very helpful.

—As parents we might look forward to the days when our children are able to integrate our norms, values and boundaries into their lives. When will it happen?

—That won't happen until the children are around four or five years old. Many parents have far too high expectations. They wonder why it is necessary to say things over and over again. That is just the way it is. In some families and institutions, punishment is part of the way children are raised. When punishing, all you end up with is children who are able to live up to what is expected of them because they are afraid of the punishment. I believe that punishment and reward are two sides of the same coin—and equally bad practice.

Family Time

—*Some families and institutions believe in rewarding children when they do what is right and expected of them instead of punishing them when they get it wrong.*

—Rewarding children works just fine when we are talking about a performance, say at school or on the sporting field. When we are talking about behavior however, rewarding children is completely wrong. Punishments as well as rewards make it impossible for children to build a sense of self-worth. Instead they will only learn what the adults want from them. They will soon be able to sense when their parents are happy but they won't learn much about themselves.

The most positive experience a child can have is a *personal response*. It is one thing to praise a child and something completely different to send a personal message. There is a huge difference between saying: "You are so wonderful!" and "I am so pleased you did this!" To be wonderful is an ideal. In time, the child will conclude that life is about being wonderful. The consequences of their actions and how these impact on others doesn't matter that much. This fosters very antisocial children and their focus in life will be centered around performances and achievements. Parents need to ask themselves how they can communicate on a more personal level and deliver more personal messages.

> *There is a huge difference between saying: "You are so wonderful!" and "I am so pleased you did this!" To be wonderful is an ideal. In time, the child will conclude that life is about being wonderful. The consequences of their actions and how these impact on others doesn't matter that much.*

—It is challenging for parents when children aren't able to do things the first time around. They get angry, frustrated, sad and give up. How can we motivate our children and show them that they don't have to get it right straight away?

—Children who are seeking perfection will often have copied this from their parents. If the children are used to seeing a mother who is able to do everything and get everything right then they will think that life is like that and that they also have to succeed in everything they do.

My son refused to write essays when he was young—until we worked out what was happening. Hundreds of times my wife and I had been sitting around the dinner table and he had seen me getting up saying: "Wait a minute, I just have to finish something!" I would leave the table, finish what I was writing and return. My son thought that this was how you did things: pick up a pen and a piece of paper and finish things in no time. He obviously couldn't do it as quickly as I did so he thought he couldn't do it at all. When we realized what was happening I taught him how to write an essay and it was no longer a problem.

—One of the most difficult things for parents is to let go and resist falling into the trap of searching for perfection. Children must be able to make mistakes, even though it is frustrating and we would like to help them so they get it right first time around.

—If we compare childhood with a marathon then many parents try to run the distance for their children. Parents find it difficult to accept that their children get frustrated because it sounds like they are unhappy. Behind this lies the reality that many parents don't like getting frustrated themselves. Everything has to go smoothly and we try to succeed in everything we do. If we are unable to do it then it is either impossible to do or not worth doing. When parents turn into *service parents* who think they are helping their children they are in fact creating children who are helpless. Along the marathon of childhood parents ought to put up some pit-stops and then let their children do the running. At the pit-stops they can offer something to drink, a motivation or whatever else is needed.

Helplessness and lack of personal competence shows itself very clearly in puberty. At that age far too many contemplate suicide, become depressed, aggressive and take drugs because they lack basic life competencies. Parents who don't accept their children's frustrations during childhood are self-centered because frustration is part of every learning-process. It is both natural and necessary.

—In a relationship it is more rewarding to be confirmed that the chemistry is right than it is to be praised. I would prefer to hear that my partner enjoys being with me than to hear if he thinks I am beautiful. Do you think children feel like that too?

—Sure, and the wonderful part is that we are able tell our children what happens inside of us when we are with them. Tell them how our relationship makes us feel.

I actually don't think it is a good idea to praise children for doing things that are natural for them to do, such as going to the toilet by themselves. However, this has become many parents' rather stereotypical way of expressing their love. I recommend that you use different words. Praise releases endorphins—a hormone which creates a brief feeling of happiness or satisfaction—just like shopping does. We can become highly dependent on that. As a result the child will walk around craving praise and therefore develop an emotional need to be at the centre of attention.

—Does this mean that instead of telling the child he is good at throwing the ball, we should register what he does and say: "I can see that you are enjoying yourself!"

—Much better! By doing that you are giving him something very important: you make it easier for him to speak about his own emotions. The art of living in a family is all about converting loving feelings into loving behavior. Just because we do something out of love it might not come across like that to others. Little children love to be praised—and it is indeed also wonderful to be able to praise someone else. Praise is generally perceived as something worthwhile. To find out if praise is worthwhile try to test it by saying the same thing to your partner. If my wife comes home every day and tells me how good I am at cooking I would soon lose my appetite. It would be something completely different if she let me know how much she enjoys the food or tells me how happy she is that I like cooking. These are *personal messages*, which strengthen our relationship and gives me the motivation to continue—not only the cooking but also the relationship.

> *Praise gives us a "warm" feeling. It releases endorphins—the hormones that create a brief feeling of happiness or satisfaction. What it doesn't do, is build on the rapport between adults and children simply because it is very asymmetrical—one part gives the other a positive comment.*

—What happens when a child grows up with a lot of praise? Some praise is good, isn't it?

—Of course! Praise ought to be part of the child's achievements at school, at sport, when playing music, etc. Then, praise does no harm at all—unless we are overdoing it. *What* we say is important but it is more important *how* we say it and *why* we say it—our reason or motivation for saying it. Handing out praise has become the way many parents express their love for their children—in some cases it is the only way. This is shallow and not nearly as constructive as personal observations or comments. Praise gives us a "warm" feeling. It releases endorphins—the hormones that create a brief feeling of happiness or satisfaction. What it doesn't do, is build on the rapport between adults and children simply because it is very asymmetrical—one part gives the other a positive comment. This is not an equal relationship.

Many popular parenting programs use and recommend praise but it only works as a calculated manipulation which serves to encourage certain behaviors, namely behaviors that the parents prefer. Praise as a method fosters highly insecure young people. Eventually they become adults who are dependent upon constant affirmation by their surroundings. They struggle to build a healthy feeling of self-worth and thereby an intrinsic ability to assess their choices and actions.

If your aim is to send a quick message to your child, praise does no harm but it doesn't tell your child anything about who you are. Consequently, praise is only the second best option. My advice is that you consider the following: "Why do I praise?", "What would I like to achieve?" and "Could I possibly have said something more personal?" We need to remember that praise doesn't strengthen a child's or a parent's self-worth. It is only building their self-confidence.

When parents and other adults tell a boy that he is a world champion at everything he does, then he will be in for a big surprise when he meets the real world. Out there he will realize that he isn't the only "world champion". Parents who praise like that don't do their children any favors. They will not be able to accept that real life will hurt now and then, that disappointments occur and that sadness is a natural part of living. When those children form their own relationships they are tempted to separate as soon as they have a conflict.

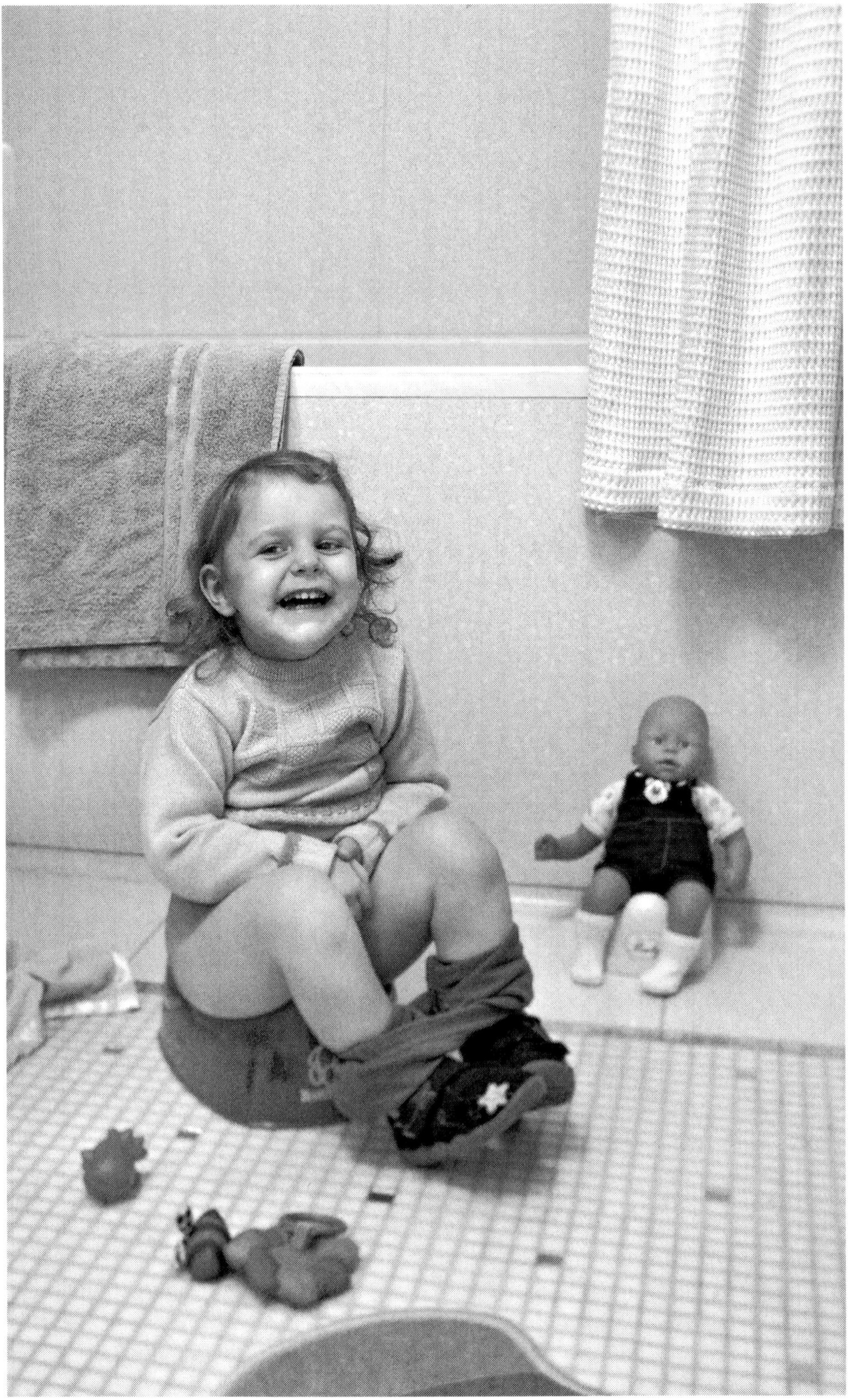

Family Time

—*Many parents grew up being told: "You are a nice girl!" or "You are a good boy!" When did this kind of judgment begin?*

—This really started in the beginning of the 1960s. Those were the days when everyone realized that criticizing children damaged their souls. Not just the harsh criticism, but any kind, because children take all of it personally. Back then the logic was: if criticism is wrong then praise must be good. Praise is indeed good if it comes from a coach or a mentor. Mind you, praise is less dangerous for adults than it is for children, and it isn't that bad when it comes from people other than parents. Interestingly, children hardly ever copy their parents' praise. You will rarely hear children praise each other.

—*Are you able to give me an example? When should I say: "I" instead of "You"?*

—Instead of saying: "You are a good girl!" or "You cannot have been very good at school since things aren't going so well!" Try to say: "It is a pleasure to see how well things are going for you." or "I got a surprise. I had the impression that things went well at school but that doesn't seem to be the case. What is this about?" You can show interest and be curious instead of simply defining children by pointing out that they are one way or another. It is important not to label them. Don't put them in a box.

Most children have a special and perhaps closer contact with one of their parents. Shared interest, shared personality traits and similar likes and dislikes might be some of the reasons why. This however, doesn't necessarily mean that the relationship with the other parent isn't good.

—*Is it always the case that a child has a special connection to one of the parents?*

—I wouldn't say "always" but most children will feel they are closest to one or the other. This isn't solely about feelings, neither is it dependent on the amount of time they spend together. It is about how a child uses one of the parents as a teacher or mentor to work out how to deal with things in life. It is a contact on an existential level. Many parents will experience different feelings when their parents die. When one dies it is very sad but when the other dies they feel completely alone in the world. This could be the other way around depending on who dies first. It has to do with this special connection.

—Parents are under a lot of pressure from society and their surroundings to raise children who are good at everything and best at most things. We compare all the time and this fosters a lot of jealousy.

—When parents feel they are under pressure they need to look in the mirror and say: "Is it my child or is it society's child?" Experts and politicians always come up with ideas that are more or less intelligent and not always true. They either want to prevent certain behaviors, bring up your children or do other things to them but there is no real reason to trust what they say—let alone do as they suggest. Look at all the focus on overweight children—this isn't about a genuine concern for the individual child. It is all about the possibility of saving on health costs. Again and again you have to remind yourself that your children are in fact *your* children, not your neighbor's, not your mother-in-law's and not the institution's children. You have to set the agenda. Focus on how you and your children are doing. Prioritize your interactions. This is, and always should be, more important than whatever someone else might think or say.

—Children are all different and we are not able to guide them equally. Parents often worry about their children: are they normal, good enough, do they get enough stimulation . . . ?

Family Time

—Sure, parents do worry—often too much! We receive many letters from parents who are concerned because their children only have two good friends. I wonder what is wrong with having just two friends? Many children don't have any at all but it is as if we have to have many friends. It is seen as some kind of criteria for success. Let me say this: "There should be only one important ambition for parents: get to know your own children as best you can."

Due to external pressures we often end up focusing on our children's limitations instead of developing their potential. For more than 30 years I have worked with adults of all ages. You can take any group of these people and listen to their life stories and you will realize that a *normal childhood* does not exist. Nobody goes through childhood without hurts and scars.

> *There should be only one important ambition for parents: get to know your own children as best you can.*

The worst term coined during the 1980s was *well-functioning families*. This means absolutely nothing and completely lacks substance. Nobody is able to define what it means to be *well-functioning*. It is an important term for governments because families who don't "function well" are a drain on their resources. For the government, the cheaper a family is to run the more *well-functioning* it is. The more talk there is about *well-functioning families* the more pressure parents are under and the more important it is for us all to have *well-functioning children*. Consequently, the more things go wrong.

I think you need to hit back if a carer or teacher tells you that your children are *well-functioning*. With a touch of humor, I suggest you say: "Well . . . If you can't say anything positive about my child then I don't want to hear anything at all." If we were to look at people who have something interesting to contribute, those who make a difference to society and have a positive impact on their families and friends, then we will realize that hardly any of them were *well-functioning* as children.

—In my experience it is difficult to feel good about life until I feel good about myself. It is easy to feel good when people say nice things but at the end of the day you have to trust your own judgments. How can parents help their children develop that understanding?

—That is one of the dilemmas of psychology. There is no real answer, as it is an ideological question. Ideologists would say that, when it comes to children, it is better to play than to compete. This has some very deep cultural roots. When a child runs out onto the sports field proclaiming: "Yeah, I am the best!" then it will become a problem. Many children don't want to be part of the game because they fear that they can't cope. This fear becomes evident on the sporting field when the main focus turns to the achievement rather than participation. Some children believe they have to perform and be the best to be able to participate. This, to a great extent, is related to the kinds of parents they have. The parents might be anxious or simply have very high expectations.

—What can parents do? Expect less? Be less anxious?

—I don't believe it is possible to adopt an attitude, which is less anxious overnight. What I would recommend is to consider whether or not you trust and have faith in your children. Worries are not constructive. Trust, on the other hand, is a highly precious gift. Parents who have expectations about their children's academic and sporting achievements must obviously make sure that these expectations reflect the children's abilities and talents. It might be somewhat complicated assessing what their real abilities are because they are so focused on living up to their parents' expectations. Should it happen that children perform below their abilities it might be time to consider the expectations versus the children's abilities and their interests. If these two do not correspond then it is a good idea to acknowledge: "Fine, that is the way they are." Sooner or later they will have to work it out for themselves anyway.

It is every parent's duty to love their children exactly the way they are. Imagine if your child is physically unable to perform then you might spend a lot of time surfing the net trying to find some kind of cure or treatment. Meanwhile, your child will develop a real sense that you think they are a big problem—a feeling that will only worsen.

I have had a conversation with a family whose seven year old son had lost his hair. His parents were worried that their son would be bullied and not be socially accepted without his hair. They found a specialist in Germany who was able to give him a hair implantation. When I met the family, the boy broke down before I had a chance to say anything. He said to his parents: "Why can you only see the hair that I don't have?" He no longer felt he existed as a person. The most important thing for the parents was his hair—or in other words: everything he was not. That is what happens when parents focus on their children's problems and become helpers who will do everything they can to solve a problem.

—Most parents will do whatever it takes to ensure their children are content and happy. It is indeed difficult to see that we at times have to live with pain. How can parents ensure that they focus not only on the problems?

—This can be done by assessing how much energy is used on a specific problem compared with the energy used on the rest of their existence and qualities. It is also important to be aware of the fact that when we are helping a child we are also supporting our own self-confidence. While this might make us feel good, the child's self-confidence, on the other hand, is being hurt. As a rule of thumb: we should never do anything for our children that they are capable of doing themselves.

> *As a rule of thumb: we should never do anything for our children that they are capable of doing themselves.*

—I wonder how we are able to motivate anxious children—those who are afraid of trying different things and meeting new people?

—That isn't possible. All you can do is sit with them and give them a hug. You might say: "It must be terrible for you to be so afraid. I wish I could wave a magic wand so you wouldn't be scared, but I can't." That is something you can say but you certainly shouldn't try to motivate them. If you do that, you will, in fact, be focusing on their anxiety and thereby turn it into a problem. The child will feel like a real burden and will take on some unreasonable guilt. They will think: "It is my fault that my parents are worried about me. If only I wasn't so afraid my parents would be happy." That's why you must never turn it into a project.

—But many parents do worry. They might have a two year old son who is a bit more shy than other children. He is not able to relax at a dance class but when the mother asks him if he had a good time, he says: "Yes!" How can they support him so he can handle the situation?

—Trust! Have confidence in him and believe him when he says he had a good time. Some children are more sensitive than others, they can't handle chaos and panic when they have to go somewhere—such as a birthday party. They are unable to play with more than two to three children at a time.

My son found it very difficult to attend birthday parties. The rule at his school was that everyone or nobody should be invited to a birthday party.

—*That is still the rule in some places.*

—I believe it is wrong. Some children don't feel comfortable with many children around and the chaos that inevitably is part of a birthday party. We can start analyzing this and turn it into a psychological case study but what good would that do? Some women like it when men flirt with them, while others find it uncomfortable. That isn't really a problem. People are just different.

—*Would a religious faith be of support in case the parents fail? Can religion give some answers and help children feel comfortable, trust themselves as well as build their self-esteem?*

—That really does depend on whether or not the religion means something personal or it is more of a philosophical approach. Is it a spiritual experience or is it something learned? Psychology has predominantly been concerned with the questions of how various religions restrict our abilities to develop emotionally. Mind you, there is a distinct difference between religion and spirituality. Deep down, spirituality is all about self-esteem, self-realization and personal development. Religion represents a good example or a symbol of how children relate to their parents' values in general. When children reach a certain age many of them are allowed to test different religious values. Children should be influenced by their parents' culture and faith as long as it isn't forced upon them against their will and they are not punished if they are unable to identify with that particular faith. When children and young people develop and define their personalities they obviously look at who and what they would like to be—but just as much of this is about who and what they don't want to be. Many young people distance themselves from religion, yet, they might pick it up again when they get a sense of their personal freedom from the age of 20.

Prayer can certainly provide comfort in certain situations. Many children pray when they need help or when the people they love need help. They also pray for international and natural disasters or tragedies. If you are a religious family it is important to remind them of this option and perhaps pray with them. We must also acknowledge our own limitations. We need to tell them that we don't have answers and solutions to everything: "There might be a solution to that, but I don't know. I can't answer your question." Reality is that there are no answers to certain questions.

Many psychotherapists, psychologists and psychiatrists try to analyze and define the characteristics of families whose children have eating disorders. I don't operate like that. I never do any work in advance before meeting a new family. Neither do I compare or draw reference to families with similar issues or comparable situations. Not even if two families have similar symptoms—in fact, then I pay much greater attention to their differences than their similarities. This is not about fanatical individualism, it is about *acknowledging* people's individualities—especially in the areas where stereotyping tends to dominate.

—This requires parents to be able to consider religion as a set of values rather than an admonishing doctrine and ideology. Isn't it about the children being allowed to wonder and ponder about the mysteries of life? Why do I feel the way I do? Why am I sad or happy, scared, content and what is it that makes me feel guilty? This kind

of spiritual relationship and connection might give them a sense of freedom without being held accountable for everything. Instead, they will be able to have a spiritual conversation about the things that are on their mind.

—Relating to religion with such maturity will first and foremost help prevent anxiety. Secondly, it will provide children with an identity. If you arrive in a different country you will need to get to know the religious beliefs of that culture to be able to integrate and function properly. In the western world science is a "religion" and this is a language others must learn in order for them to be able to understand us. Experiences are rather useless when it comes to making important political decisions. Only research matters and experiences have become something which we commercialize. We sell experiences instead of sharing them.

Many parents make similar observations and wonder: "The world my children grow up in is distinctly different to the world I grew up in. Do my experiences have any value at all? Are they still valid?" You have to take the essence of your values and tailor these for the next generation. You might not necessarily "speak their language" but you must at least ensure that you make your language understandable.

> *The world my children grow up in is distinctly different to the world I grew up in. Do my experiences have any value at all? Are they still valid?*

—*When we ponder some of life's big questions we learn about humility. All religious belief system do focus on humility—just the fact that we don't know the end result.*

—Children will learn about humility by having humble parents. This doesn't necessarily depend on their religious belief—or whether they have one at all. It depends on how you as a parent look at the world, at other people and at your own life. Talking about it doesn't do much good.

Focus and concentration is often an important part of a religious culture. When a majority of children these days are unable to either focus or concentrate it has very little to do with alleged emotional problems. Children are not able to focus simply because they have never been taught how.

—Were child care centers and kindergartens to introduce periods of meditation many parents would protest because this is associated with Buddhism. Instead of looking at it as a way of relaxing and focusing. How can we support children's spiritual journeys without upsetting some parents?

—How do we build on the goodness which is inside all children? First they have to discover their intrinsic friendliness. Parents, teachers, politicians, police and others complain that we are too stressed. We simply have far too many projects and are too focused on being successful. All of this we transfer to our children. We might get away with a label and call it *over-stimulation* but the point is: children can't cope. Some call it *stress* and in a highly simplified way explain that when parents are stressed then their children will also be stressed.

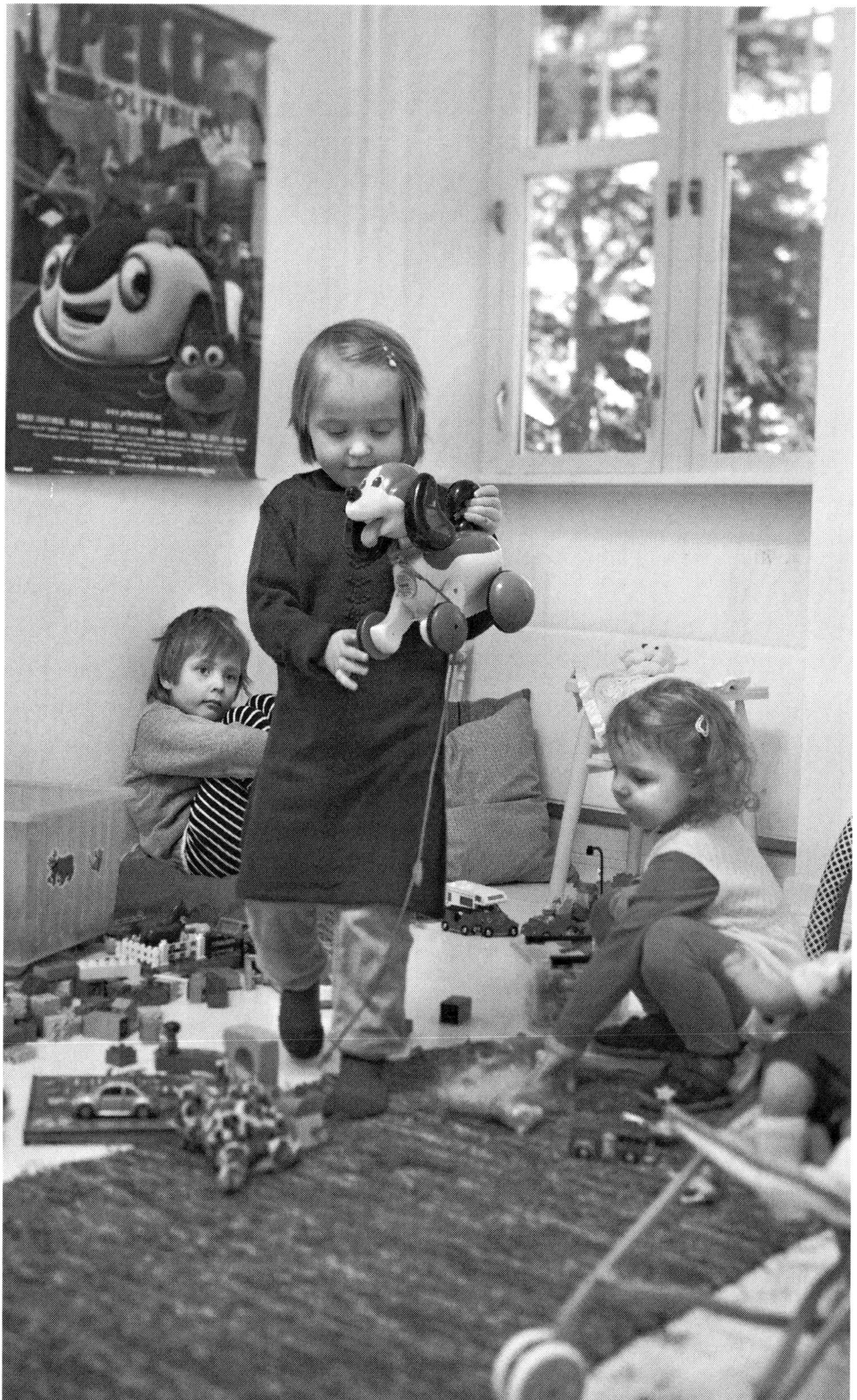

A group of 13 and 14 year old children learned to work with axes. The axes were almost as big as the children. Safety concerns and insurance policies would normally put a stop to even thinking about this but the children were allowed to chop large pieces of wood right through the middle. When they were able to gather enough internal strength through breathing exercises they could do things they never thought possible. As it turned out, the children were able to transfer this self-control and focus to mathematics, amongst other things. Another group of 11 and 12 year old children were taken to the beach and each placed on their own rock. They were given a notebook and in case they became really restless they could write down their thoughts. Or they could just sit still for 30 minutes. After the exercise the children were surprised to learn how wonderful it was that everything around them was quiet and what happened to them when there was no one to talk to so they could just sit and let their thoughts roll. They had never experienced anything like that before. We need to remember this because children do need silence as well as the opportunity to wonder—they need time away from the daily stress. This is very similar to what people of any religious belief experience when they pray or meditate. It is a closeness to nature, the universe and indeed life itself.

—*You say we need time out from the daily stress. How do we know that our children are stressed and what is it that stresses them?*

—In older children you will notice when they find it difficult to sit still and focus. They might only be able to focus for shorter periods of time. They might also find it difficult to fall asleep and have frequent nightmares. If they find it difficult to play by themselves or they struggle to absorb themselves in whatever they do, they might be stressed. Something, which stresses children is their parents' insecurity. Children obviously know if their parents continually stress and worry about things like: "Help! How do I get the children to sleep? Which method did I read about last week? What did the woman in the mothers' group say? Maybe I am a bad mother because I can't get my children to sleep . . . !" This kind of stress will also stress the children.

> *We must be prepared to allow our lives to be enriched by our children. We must learn from the good and from the not so good.*

—*What else can we do to raise children who are not stressed?*

—An important factor is a healthy dose of self-esteem. This in turn means peace of mind and confidence which is something parents can help with. Children need to get to know themselves and develop the ability to read the signals their bodies send them. Two considerations are important:

1. "What do I know about myself?"
2. "How do I relate to what I know about myself?"

Children are highly sensitive and will quickly copy adults and the ways in which they relate to themselves. If you as a parent criticize and blame yourself then they will do exactly the same. As human beings we are neither positive nor negative, *we are!* Children's self-esteem is strengthened when they know their parents value them. To avoid stressed and unhappy children we must be prepared to allow our lives to be enriched by our children. We must learn from the good and from the not so good.

What makes children and the whole family harmonious? Some argue that routines are important so they know what is going to happen. I personally like to be organized, prioritize what has to be done and structure homework and play. Even watching film, reading books—bed time stories in particular—all come with some kind of predictability.

—Are daily routines the key to a harmonious child?

—I need to point out that this depends on the culture you live in. Most of the world's children sleep perfectly well without bed time stories or songs. There is however, no doubt that reading to them develops their language and their own interest in reading. They might not be too interested in reading between the ages of eight to fifteen or twenty but it will come back. In some countries parents are strongly encouraged to read to their children and as a result their reading and writing improves dramatically. It helps to hear a language frequently—and not just the spoken word. Good children's books are in fact literature and all children benefit from listening to good literature.

—Many parents are very busy. In the evenings some tend to switch onto autopilot. Some might read or play music for 30 minutes or perhaps less. Often this becomes a routine they struggle to get through because they are so tired. Is that alright?

—Children are grateful little beings. They feel like they are in heaven whenever either the mother or father sits by their bed reading to them—even though they would in fact prefer to be in their own bed.

Communicating with your child, on the other hand, is easiest done when you are doing something together. You can't just sit with them and say: "Now, let's talk about our relationship!" Many children enjoy just hanging out, pottering and chatting. This does vary from child to child and might change during different stages of their lives.

Family Time

—Parents often do things with the children—even though they might not really feel like it. They can play sport, build LEGO, play board games, etc. whilst their minds are elsewhere. It is easy to multi-task and be with he children and at the same time read the paper, check text messages, cook dinner, etc. We are physically there but not mentally. Keeping in mind the debate about quality time and quantity time, should we really stop and focus?

—If you are not mentally there it is probably best not to play with your child. We shouldn't forget that some adults do find it difficult to play with children—either because they have never tried before or because their inner child has left them. I personally felt very awkward for a couple of years and literally had to get my son to teach me again. I didn't have any role models in my family but I was acutely aware that my son wasn't interested in that excuse—he just wanted to play. As a general rule, I think it is important that we make sure not to turn play into a duty. Just play with your child and try to find some meaning. If playing with toy cars, dolls or LEGO doesn't feel meaningful to you then perhaps just being with your child does?

> *I think it is important that we make sure not to turn play into a duty. Just play with your child and try to find some meaning.*

—In literature about children and their upbringing there is a considerable focus on play—and the fact that they develop important skills through play. It is said that parents need to encourage a variety of different playing activities, participate actively and give praise along the way. What is your opinion about that?

—Yes, I have heard that too. It does depend on how we define *play*. What parents describe as *playing* is for the children a way of *learning*. Children and researchers learn in similar ways. They both come up with ideas, theories and experiments.

It is important for children that their parents are part of these activities—but the children must be the driving force. This might not be important for the actual activity but it is the only way children can spend time with their parents—on their terms. Everyone's level, skills and abilities are equal. I don't believe parents should use play as a pedagogical tool or technique in an attempt to teach them something. Use play as one of the many ways through which you can spend time together and get to know each other on a personal level.

—*How about those children who don't feel comfortable playing by themselves, those who always need their parents there?*

—There are many children between the ages of one and three who want their parents to play with them. The parents should do it for as long as they think it is enjoyable or they can find the time to do it. Around 30 minutes a day would be ideal.

—*When we spend time together as a family it often happens on the adults' terms.*

—In that regard, children basically need two things:

1. To spend time with other children who are of similar ages so they can play, explore, and challenge themselves physically as well as intellectually.
2. They also need to learn how to be adults. This, they cannot learn from child carers or schoolteachers. Sure, they are adults, but they also get paid for being with your children, and as you know, they are not your children's parents. It becomes equally complicated if you try to be a teacher yourself. Then

your children won't spend much time with genuine adult role models. Consequently, it is important for you not to try too hard to be *a parent* or *a teacher*. You must allow yourself to be an adult and do adult things, such as lie on the lounge for a while, read the paper, flirt with your partner, trim the roses and other things that give meaning to your life. This is how your children will learn to be adult.

We have found that since the early 1990s a large portion of parents don't really want to be or behave like adults. They want to be young forever partly because they don't know how to be adults, as they had no real role models. We have seen some interesting examples of highly skilled tradespeople being invited to kindergartens and schools. A carpenter for example, might start making a piece of furniture and the children will look on for hours without getting bored. Parents must take the leadership role and do things they want to do. Say: "Listen, we are going for a bike ride." Their children might complain but then you say: "No problem. I am going anyway, would you like to join me?" Don't stay at home just because the child doesn't want to go. If you stay at home you will hand over the leadership mantle to them. The problem is that they don't know what is good for them until they have tried.

—You strongly suggest that children learn personal and social responsibility. They have to work out when they are hungry and tired. At the same time you say that parents have to show leadership and say that a certain day is a "family day" or that it is time to go for a bike ride or whatever it is.

—Yes, this is necessary. We are exposed to plenty of different and often opposing pedagogical theories, but none of these argue against parents showing leadership. Children need *parental leadership*. Without this, they will not thrive. The father who interacts with his son once a month by taking him to a club or a bar must obviously find another way of showing leadership. It has to be relevant leadership, which is not only about the parents. Children who are nearing their teenage years are not easily tempted by their parents and their suggestions. They are quite capable of working out for themselves what is best for them. They have to experiment and you will be able to find out how much they have learned at home—sometimes you learn this the hard and painful way.

Children need parental leadership. Without this, they will not thrive.

—*Some children want to be part of activities but are a bit reluctant as well. They want to take part so they stay, on the other hand they don't want to take part, so they look on and make rude remarks and maybe obstruct the activity. I have heard parents tell them that they behave like spoiled children when they don't get things their way. Then the children start crying.*

—The very moment parents use their power and attach labels to their children they will cry. It is hurtful to be told what you are like when it is defined by your behavior. The parents in your example could have said: "Listen, I get very angry when you sabotage something I would like to do just because you don't want to do it. I want you to either participate or not participate." That's it, say no more. The child knows where you stand.

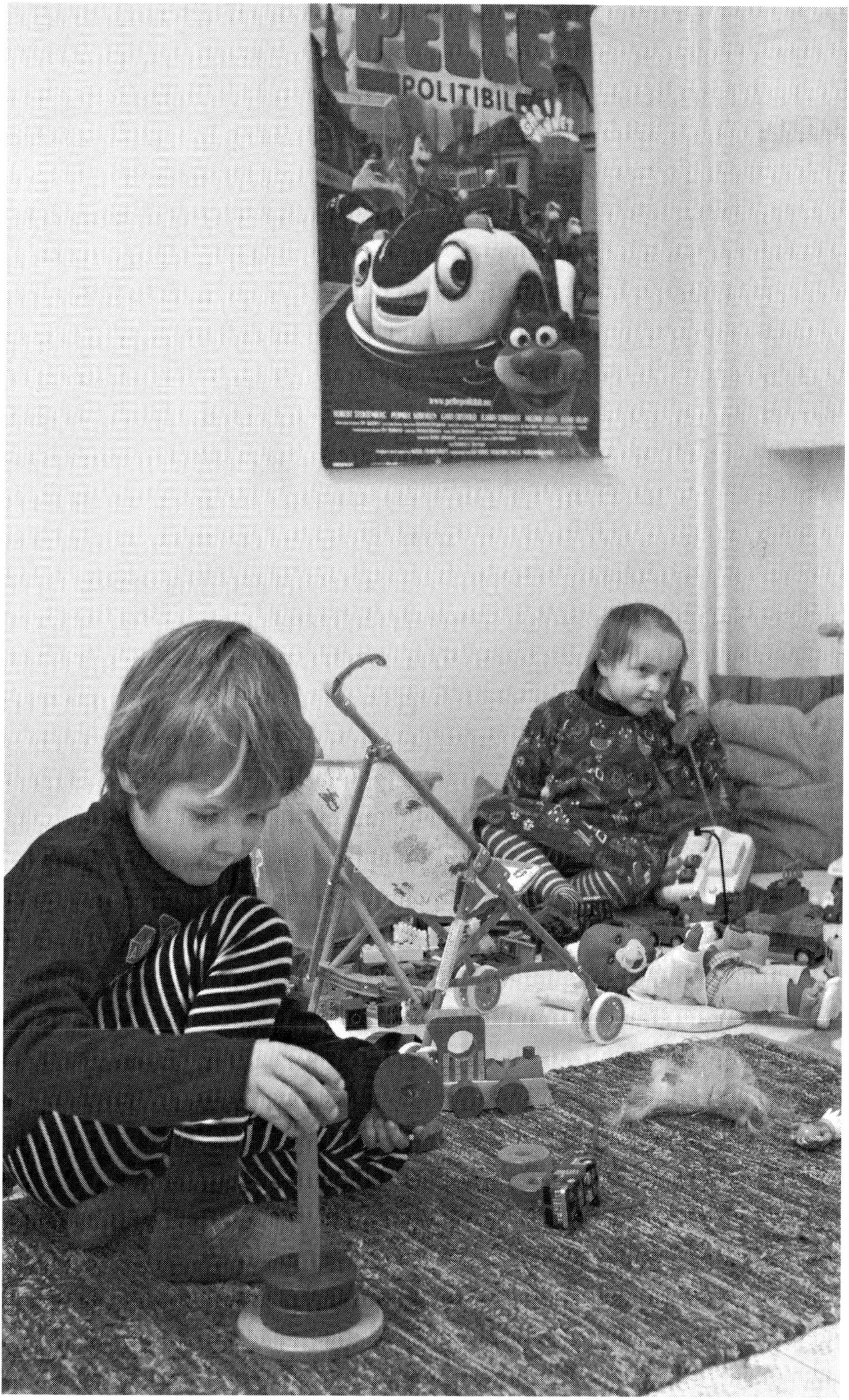
POLITIBIL

—You think two sentences or less are enough to say most things?

—Absolutely! Anything more than that will be either moralizing or criticizing—or both. It is like trying to shoot a sparrow with a pump gun. Most children will get caught between the genuine loyalty they have for their parents and their search for personal independence. They need to know and understand that it is alright to be independent. This is why one of the most important things a family can do is to allow each other to say: "No!"—and help and support each other to say it. Children must feel it is alright to not participate without worrying about their parents becoming sad because of it.

—Yet, many children find it difficult to say: "No!" both at home and outside of the home. Maybe it is difficult to say: "No!" when someone wants to borrow a football because they don't want to exclude or be excluded. How can a child become better at saying: "No!"?

—I suggest that children start practicing at home. Before they can say: "No!" to their friends they must be able to say it at home. But before they are able to say: "No!" to others they must be able to say: "Yes!" to themselves. When we become parents we are often confronted by our own upbringing. As parents we really don't know what our children find challenging about our behavior. If you would like to know how you are as a parent you will have to accept that they will let you know in dribs and drabs. You will find out when you see how your children are coping and dealing with challenges. You will also get some indications when you observe their first serious relationship. You will get an even clearer picture when your children become parents themselves. Finally, you might get the full picture when you turn 80 years old.

If you want to know how you are as a parent you could ask your children to write down the three worst things about you as a parent.

We once received a letter from a teenager who in an e-mail had written to his first girlfriend: "My mother is a whore and a bitch!" He felt that this statement was nothing more than a way of expression and that it didn't mean much. But what did it mean? Well, he had something to say to his mother, which he had repressed because he didn't want to hurt her. Should he be criticized for saying it? No! The girlfriend was the boy's first serious relationship and he was telling her something about what he had felt during his childhood. Sure, the mother might have a different interpretation but his expression was part of a bigger picture and a way for him to let go and release some pressure.

—Would you be able to comment on children's abilities to take responsibility—or to understand responsibility? My children don't live in a hotel, they have to chip in because we as parents can't do everything.

—Responsibilities can be categorized into two different groups—and these are hugely different:

1. Social responsibility towards other people.
2. Personal/existential responsibility for ourselves and our own lives.

Children have not yet developed their own values in the same way adults have. Nevertheless, they can take responsibility for themselves from an early age. They will form opinions, have wishes and develop their personal styles very early in life. They know what kind of hairstyle they like, what they want to wear, what they want to eat and which games they like to play. All this can and should be their responsibility. Just remember, children can do many things themselves but not necessarily on their own. It is about advising and guiding them rather than manipulating and forcing them to do things.

As parents we have to be ready for when our children are ready to assume greater responsibility. This happens when they start complaining that we as parents decide too much or when they insist that they want to make more decisions for themselves. When conflicts around this become destructive it is often an indication that you are indeed making too many decisions on behalf of your children.

For centuries, the reality of raising children has been that parents were responsible for their children. This could only work as long as the parents had absolute authority and were prepared to threaten or punish their children when this authority was challenged. These days, children's *social responsibility* within the family, at childcare and at school has become increasingly important. We emphasize that they have a responsibility towards other people as well as for their property. This is obviously wonderful, as it is this kind of society we want to live in. What we have forgotten though, is to help them learn how to take that *personal responsibility*. We expect this of them but have not allowed them to learn it. Consequently, there is an unmet need for this.

—I see parents who get angry when their children forget their bags, keys or whatever. They blame the children in spite of the fact that they have never given them the opportunity to be responsible for their own things.

—Many parents do too much for their children. At the end of the day, it is obviously the parents' responsibility that their children have the keys to the home—but they shouldn't lecture. They need to state what happened, that it wasn't right and that things can be different: "In case you lose your phone and can't find it you'll have to buy a new one!" or "If you forget your wallet somewhere then you will have lost your money!" They will obviously be annoyed because they'll expect a service where you fix it for them—as usual. Incidentally, this also happens in relationships—often service and love are seen as similar and inseparable.

This also applies when your children refuse to help out at home. You can say: "Listen, if you think there is a community somewhere in the world where you don't have to contribute, then you are welcome to find it and move there. In this place you are not able to live without contributing." I haven't yet met anyone who hasn't responded to that. When the message is clear and definite—and it comes from the heart without a moral judgment—then things will happen.

> *Listen, if you think there is a community somewhere in the world where you don't have to contribute, then you are welcome to find it and move there. In this place you are not able to live without contributing.*

—*Who holds the responsibility for tidying the kids' rooms? Can we expect this of our children?*

—Yes . . . with certain reservations. Think about yourself and your partner. Is the housekeeping a chore or something you enjoy? Your attitude influences your children's attitude. Children are not born with an automatic indicator telling them when their room needs to be tidied. Parents need to tell small children: "Wow! This place needs to be tidied. We need to get things off the floor and on the shelves and in the drawers. I think I better help you do it sometime tomorrow." When the child is six, seven or eight years old you say: "I just saw your room and I think it is very messy. If it was my room I would clean it up. Let me know if you need my help." It isn't a good idea to start an argument or tell them they might as well learn how to tidy a room now because they will have to do it when they grow up. By the way, some children automatically tidy their room all by themselves. Whatever they do, don't worry too much because when they grow a bit older and fall in love they will most certainly tidy up before their partner comes over.

—*How much can we expect of our children? And should they get paid for helping at home?*

—In a society where most families have money I think children have a right to some amount of pocket money. I can't tell you how much but the family's economic situation and how much their friends get should play a part of that consideration. I don't believe children should be given pocket money as a salary—it shouldn't be given as a reward either. If you are going to pay a child for baby-sitting a younger sibling or for cleaning the bathroom then the amount should be negotiated with them. When my son turned seven he came to offer his services when he needed extra money for something. That was good.

Traditionally speaking, pocket money only featured in the lives of the upper classes. Their aims were two-fold:

1. To teach their children the value of money by letting them work for it.
2. They had enough money so why not share it with the children?

Which of these aims are more effective I cannot say but I can tell you that it is a mistake giving children money as a symbol of your love or because you want to buy peace and calm. This will inevitably go wrong. It is absolutely possible to grow up and develop a sound and responsible relationship to money in both affluent and non-affluent families. It depends on your attitude to money.

Family Time

I think children have a right to some amount of pocket money—but I don't believe it should be given as a salary or a reward.

—*Is there a conflict between us being good parents and our desire to keep up appearances?*

—I will have to make a rather unpopular and perhaps unexpected statement: today's social pressure on families is less than it has ever been. Think of living in a small community a hundred years ago! You couldn't take a step outside of the norm without being noticed and put back in your place. These days we have possibilities aplenty. Of course, parents can feel the pressure, but objectively speaking, it really shouldn't be of concern. I actually don't understand why we worry about it. Mobiles and cell phones became very popular in the early 1990s yet today people are still surprised when they see young children with them. A British psychologist argues that children should have a phone when they are six years old because it is part of their generation's social life. He is right but it does contradict some people's moral ideas. They wonder when children will learn to use their phones responsibly? They shouldn't blame the children because it will only happen when adults learn to use theirs properly.

—*I feel like a terrible mother if the house is a big mess and when we on an ordinary weekday snack instead of sitting down for dinner. We might watch a movie and I let them go to bed very late. I feel I have let go of all the boundaries and I am far too kind . . . !*

—It is never about *what* you do. It is always about *why* you do it—your motivation for doing what you do. If your motivation is laziness and you couldn't be bothered because you just want peace and calm, then things will go wrong. Your children will feel uncomfortable simply because they are being "bought". If you, on the other hand, do it because you want to have a bit of fun with the family then your children will feel that you prioritize them. That is exactly what you do because you are with them in spite of the messy house and all the other things you should be doing. We shouldn't be too perfect. It is more important that you are there for your children than for your house and your clean floors.

—How important are moral principles when conflicts arise? Should I not allow my child to have a phone, fashion brands or whatever they might want?

—Are you going to allow your *personal principles* to have a negative impact on your *personal relationships*? It is hard to imagine a child smiling and saying to his mother: "That's a really good moral principle!" I believe you need to reconsider your principles if they are damaging your relationships. In a multicultural society families will inevitably always have different lifestyles. Amongst this multitude of ways of living you will find happy and content people. There isn't one right way, although this was what our parents thought—and tried hard to achieve. Today we know that there are thousands of different ways to interact with our children—all of which are perfectly fine and acceptable. A seven year old will accept your decision regarding a phone. Yet, I don't believe a 14 year old should quietly and obediently accept your rejection. What you can do is tell him that if he wants a phone he needs to save up for it himself.

A mother told us that her 11 year old son wanted a phone. I asked her: "Did he tell you why he wanted one?" She had forgotten to ask about that. When she had asked him, she came back with the answer: "Because it is cool!" I told her that his argument didn't stack up and I would say: "No!" The quality of our relationships depends very little on *what* we do. It is much more important *how* and *why* we do it. Later, the son was able to use a series of different and much better arguments in his effort to convince his mother. Nevertheless, her moral principles were so fixed that she wasn't going to change her mind. Finally he said: "Listen, I have money in the bank and you have always said that it's up to me how I spend it. Can I use my money to buy a phone?" Suddenly, the parents were stuck between two principles and had to bite the bullet.

The quality of our relationships depends very little on what we do. It is much more important how and why we do it.

—*School requires that our children do their homework. Doesn't this contradict the idea that children have to take personal responsibility? To what extent should parents interfere in regards to when and where the homework is done?*

—I believe that homework always should be the children's responsibility. Essentially, this is an issue between the *place of work* and the *children*. Parents obviously need to encourage commitment, offer support and be there to help, but not take over the responsibility for it being done. It is really not a good idea that schools see it as the parents' responsibility to get their children to do the homework. It is, in fact, absurd and creates too many conflicts. Every night homework leads to unreasonable and unnecessary struggles in most homes. These fights fundamentally undermine the desire and willingness to learn. It makes far more sense and is more constructive for the relationship between teachers and students when the responsibility lies with the students.

It has taken a long time but finally educational research coming out of Denmark, the US and the UK provides us with concrete evidence that homework has no educational value. It is, in fact, often the opposite. Homework is a form of work that students have to undertake. For years, I have challenged the amount of hours students are expected to work before it seriously damages the development of all the other competencies, which are important in life. Schools argue that homework is a constructive way of ensuring parents' involvement during their children's school years. I believe we are far beyond decent communication when teachers manipulate parents to get involved in this way. This is however, very similar to the way it all began when parents were forced to send their children to school. Completely different relationships between teachers and students would develop if education wasn't seen as compulsory but as a right of each child and young person.

—In your opinion it is up to the child to deal with all matters relating to homework and other school projects. Are you able to predict when it will happen?

—At FamilyLab we primarily work with families who are trying to work out how to deal with these issues. It is challenging indeed and a level of frustration consequently arises. Most of the time the solution is to hand responsibility for homework over to the children—and let the school know that this has happened. As a result, children will soon feel free to ask for help when needed. Often they have specific academic questions but they will also ask for help to structure the work.

Handing over responsibility to the children doesn't mean: "From today, all of this is your responsibility!" Neither does it mean that parents shouldn't get involved at all. It does however, mean that homework is the children's responsibility and with that comes the responsibility to ask for help. Far too often parents spend a lot of energy helping out in a manner which really is designed to control what happens. It is this hidden agenda which leads to conflicts—not the homework itself. When the conflicts and frustrations escalate the parents inevitably send a very destructive message, namely that the child doesn't want to learn. Nothing could actually be farther from the truth.

When it comes to conflicts relating to homework you can very wisely *strike while the iron is cold!* Sit with your child and say: "We have had a number of conflicts and fights over your homework. I don't like it. My problem is that I feel it is my responsibility that you do well at school. Reality is however, that this responsibility is yours and your teachers'. I need some help here. Do you have any suggestions to how we can do things differently?" Then you need to listen very carefully. In a more or less subtle way they will most likely tell you why your help wasn't really all that helpful anyway.

—As a child I was allowed to ride horses, play music, go to tennis, practice gymnastics, and so forth. I was allowed to try anything I wanted. These days I wish I was able to master just one of these. How important is it to let children try out different things? It all costs money, time and involvement.

—This question brings up a number of different issues. The financial question is simple, either you can afford it or you can't.

Another question is whether or not children need to finish what they have begun. You might be able to find the answer in a dialog with them. Why do they want to stop playing football and start going to karate? Let them tell you without making any decisions for them. Many parents are actually sending ambiguous messages. You can tell them that you need some time to think it through. It is perfectly alright to let them know that you are not sure. On one hand, it is important to finish what we start. On the other hand, we shouldn't continue if we don't get much out of it. Ask them for help: "What are your reasons for doing it?" Often it turns out that they have some very good reasons. My son was really good at playing badminton. Some of the coaches exploited his talents by forcing him to participate in competitions on weekends. He didn't want to join the "competition-circus" as he called it. Make your decision based on the people who are involved and not on the basis of principles.

> *Make your decision based on the people who are involved and not on the basis of principles.*

We don't tend to seek the information where it is most readily available, namely from our children. When we do ask them they will learn to reflect and weigh up options. They will learn to make decisions based on serious considerations and to argue for the decisions they make. They will only learn this by doing it—not from being told how to do it. When my son was 16 he wanted to be a bartender. He had seen the film *Cocktail* with Tom Cruise and that was what he wanted to do. I let him have that dream and work it out for himself. What right do I have to override his dreams with my opinion about what is a good career? I showed him I was pleased with his engagement and he understood that I trusted in him.

—As a parent it is relatively easy to engage positively with the things our children do. But do we also need to have some serious conversations with them about these things?

—Absolutely! I was challenged by my son. He eventually got an apprenticeship at a hotel. One day I drove past the hotel, I hadn't seen him for three months so I stopped in to see if he was at work. He was there and we chatted for a couple of minutes. Then we both became silent. I felt an urge to say certain things to him but could feel that what I wanted to say was exactly what my own mother would have said: "How are you doing financially?", "What do you do in the evenings?" and "Who are you hanging out with?"

I resisted the temptation to ask him these things but I couldn't sleep that night. I worried that I didn't have anything to say to him. Early the next morning I was able to connect with my true feelings and I knew exactly what I wanted to say to him, namely: "I would really like to just sit here for a while and enjoy watching you go about your business, then I am happy!" But that is not something we say, although it was exactly how I felt and what would have made me happy. I actually don't think my son would have thought it would have been embarrassing. I think he would have said: "Fine!"—and perhaps been quite proud. We have to say things that might seem funny or strange if we are to break free from our stereotypical roles as parents and children. We have to be brave enough to say things which for generations haven't been part of traditional parenting. It is the only way for us to be personal and develop a *personal relationship* with our children. I could have discussed and chatted about the hotel industry for a few hours but that wouldn't have had any positive impact on our *personal relationship*. We wouldn't have had the opportunity to get to know each other any better.

—Allow me to get back to the issue of parents who set the agenda. Some children want to play computer games all the time but parents believe they need to limit this. We don't have any restriction in my home so when children come for visits they often play for a few hours. There is however, a lot of talk about the moral principles of controlling this.

—People have worried about similar issues since the radio was invented. Around the turn of the century it was all about Gameboy, then computer games, then DS . . . and so it will go on. I do acknowledge that some of these activities might be harmful but let me make it clear that children who become dependent on computer games, alcohol or whatever it might be, are children with low self-esteem. This makes them vulnerable. Adults need to engage themselves and become interested in what it is their children are doing. Ask them what makes these activities meaningful for them. Don't engage simply to control them or manipulate their actions. If you enter into a dialog you might learn that they are experiencing their first real sense of success. Computer games are something they are able to master and they might be able to communicate with others online who feel just like they do. They might feel a sense of belonging and value. It is obviously important to do something if the child is becoming addicted but remember that this addiction is a symptom—it is not the cause. Parents need to work with other aspects of their children's lives to strengthen their defense systems against addiction.

—Many separated parents struggle in the area of communication. Children whose parents don't live together often sense that there is a difference of opinion between the two households. Is it alright for a child to experience a bad relationship between the parents? What can be done about it?

—*Acknowledgement* has always been a very effective medicine. You could say to your child: "It must be challenging for you to have parents who are so silly." This is all that needs to be said. From then on it will be much easier for the child to cope with the lack of proper and clear communication. Children are also significantly different. Some will distance themselves around the ages of nine or ten. They mature very quickly—too quickly perhaps? The other end of this extreme are the parents who treat their children in an atrocious manner and they have to live with psychopaths for all or some of the time. These parents lack empathy and are extremely selfish. Everything revolves around them and they are expert manipulators. Unfortunately, it is very difficult to break free from a psychopath—especially for a child.

Acknowledgement has always been a very effective medicine. You could say to your child: "It must be challenging for you to have parents who are so silly." This is all that needs to be said. From then on it will be much easier for the child to cope with the lack of proper and clear communication.

—How can a child deal with the situation where one parent manipulates and is condescending towards the other? How much can children cope with?

—It really does hurt their self-esteem and can make them lonely. In most instances they will no longer trust adults and in some cases this can cause long term damage. When children are hurt they lose their vitality and cheerfulness. However, no damage is done when they feel a deep sense of sadness because they miss their father. This doesn't damage their personal development—it is just the way it is. The same will happen if someone they love dies. It does become unacceptable though, when one parent doesn't understand their own boundaries and ends up mixing their personal feelings for the other parent into the relationship with the children.

—In which ways can a separation become beneficial for the children?

—When parents are able to sort themselves out their children will find it much easier to get by. Children whose parents have separated might find themselves in a conflict with one of the parents. Then they might be able to offload and talk about the issue with the other. Some children might not have that option. Perhaps conflicts arise due to the separation or as a result of it. No family is perfect and it really is a difficult challenge being with some parents. If the children have been with their father for a week they might struggle to find their inner balance when they are with mother. This is alright and no harm is done. We receive letters from children who are relieved that their parents separated because they no longer have to listen to the conflicts and fights.

—*Does it hurt the children when they hear their parents fight? Will they be scared and fear divorce? It is normal for parents to disagree from time to time so how can we explain to our children that there is nothing they need to fear?*

—This depends on a number of things. Whether or not the children feel guilty or lose confidence in the relationship with their parents depends entirely on how civilized their parents are able to argue. It certainly isn't good if they argue in a primitive and offensive manner. Every child has a number of friends whose parents have separated so they are used to it and might ask their parents if they are going to separate because they argue. You might be able to answer: "No, we have no plans to separate. Sometimes, we disagree so strongly that we feel we need to raise our voices to find out if we can come to an agreement. It is also uncomfortable for us, but it isn't dangerous."

—*Some separations are inevitable and happen. At some stage the parents might enter into new relationships. Then the children will have to relate to new adults.*

—Sure. If we look at this in an existential light, then we could hope that children whose parents have separated develop the ability to take better care of themselves. They might not make the same mistakes their parents did.

—*I would like to ask about another issue relating to* belonging. *Does a child suffer if it has no siblings? Some parents feel guilty about this.*

—We assume some kind of divine status if we think we are able to determine how our family life is going to develop. I believe it is ludicrous to have another child if the purpose is to supply a sibling to the first-born. Just because some children are happy with siblings doesn't mean that they would be unhappy without. I think we need to leave this up to nature.

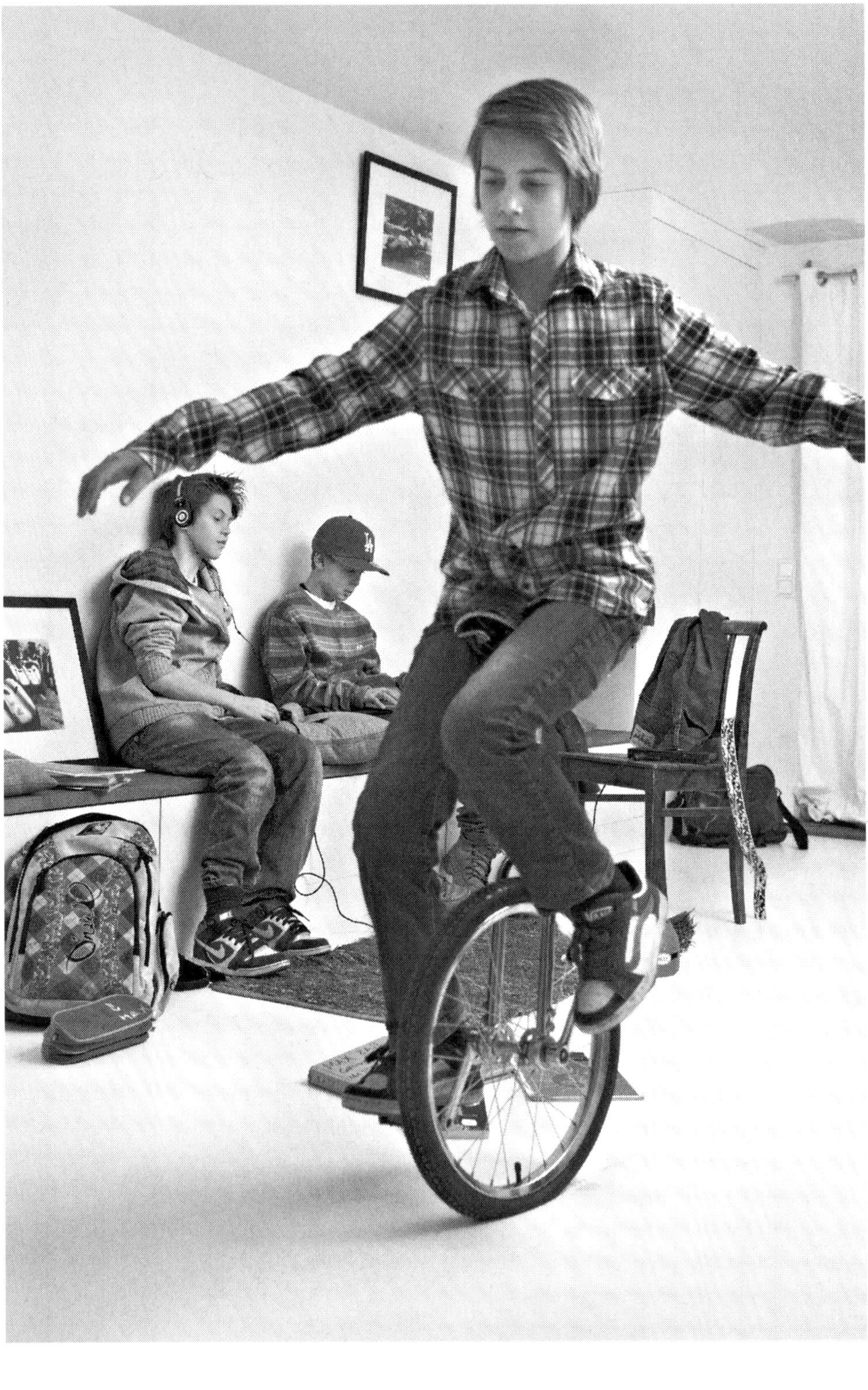

THE TEENAGER'S ROOM
– Rebellion and responsibility

It is as if young people become teenagers much earlier nowadays than they used to. I know that they are exposed to an increasing amount of images, offers and different kind of media and lifestyle options which previous generations didn't have access to. Through FaceBook®, Twitter®, YouTube®, live TV and a number of other media they can be in contact with a number of superstars on a daily basis. Moving from childhood into adulthood requires much more than a move away from home. Young people have to relate to fashion and fame, drugs and drop-outs, and many other of life's challenges. It is challenging to be a parent and realize that the teenage years are when we see the return on our investments in the earlier years.

MONICA:
—When our children reach a certain age they will be confronted with a number of serious choices. This is in relation to sex, alcohol, drugs and dropping out of school. How do we best equip teenagers to make the right choices?

JESPER:

—Our role as *parents who know everything* is over once the children reach 10 or 11 years of age. This is the time when it becomes really important that they have been trained and are able to take responsibility for themselves. They ought to know about themselves and have a good sense of self-esteem. They need this to be able to communicate clearly with friends and partners. During children's early teenage years your parental role ought to change. You should move away from being the one *who knows everything* and instead become a *sparring partner*. Many parents however, are not able to make that transition. In boxing the sparring partner plays two important roles:

1. Offers maximum opposition.
2. Does minimum harm.

When your son tells you that he has decided to buy a computer game you can find out if this is an impulse decision. As his sparring partner you could say to him: "You made a very quick decision!" or "I can tell that you have considered this carefully!" You might not agree with his decision, and you can tell him that you don't agree and would prefer he didn't buy the game, but at the end of the day, the decision is his.

To put it differently: when the children become teenagers, parents will have to acknowledge that they are *old fashioned*. This however, doesn't mean that they should let go of their norms and values. On the contrary, you ought to do whatever you can to promote these. Most parents don't realize that their opinions, attitudes and emotions have a huge impact on their teenage children. The problem is that teenagers don't want to lose face, so they don't acknowledge it and parents don't see the impact they have. Teenagers do in fact think a lot about what their parents say. They also talk to their friends about this. It is really important for you to stand up for what you believe in. What you shouldn't do is use your power to take away the freedom of youth. You have to have confidence and trust that they will do the best they can. This however, doesn't mean that they will always do what you think they ought to do.

—*This is very encouraging! What a compliment to parents to know that their teenage children use their words and wisdom when talking to their friends. "My parents are very wise but I'll do things my way anyway." This is an important vote of confidence for parents.*

—It certainly is but many parents think that the more they talk, the greater impact it has. It is in fact, the other way around. Say what you need to say in two sentences, that's all that's needed.

You have to have confidence and trust that they will do the best they can. This however, doesn't mean that they will always do what you think they ought to do.

—*We need to talk about alcohol and cigarettes. When I grew up most children were given a certain amount of money if they didn't smoke until they turned 18. Many parents still practice this and have added alcohol to the deal. It is my impression that young people experiment with alcohol at a younger and younger age. How consistent should parents be? Is the deal off if they taste a beer at a party and later tell the parents?*

—If you have such a deal in place and they have had a beer, you need to work out if this is going to be the first of many or not. This makes a difference. If you have a good relationship, they will tell you. If they would like to stick to the deal then I think it is important to say that you are ready to implement it.

—*Are these kind of rewards or carrots good? Or are they just old-fashioned tricks?*

—It is nothing but friendly manipulation. The question is, how many teenagers under the age of 18 think about the consequences of their actions? I don't believe it is useful to run a huge propaganda campaign. This only works in authoritarian communities. In any other community, propaganda has the opposite effect. A 17 year old boy had started smoking but he didn't really like it—nor did he like the new friends he hung out with. He asked his mother if she could ring his friends and tell them that she had forbidden him to spend time with them. This way, he didn't have to tell the boys and he could let his mother take the blame. Three months later the problem was solved. This obviously doesn't mean that it is a good idea for parents to ban their children from seeing their friends. What matters most, is *how* and *why* we do things—not *what* we actually do. There is always something happening back-stage, which has an impact on what is happening on stage.

Let me share an example with you. A father was the sound engineer at a place where I gave a lecture. During the break he told me that something at home had taught him a lot about his role as a father. He had been separated for years and had a 16 year old daughter who would visit him on the weekends. She would often ask for permission to do a number of different things and in an effort to remain well-liked he would often say: "Yes!" Once, when he thought she had gone to far, he said: "No!" They yelled at each other until he drove her back to her mother. Before they left she went to the bathroom and wrote with lipstick on the mirror: "Dad rules!" She was actually pleased that he had finally put his foot down. I am obviously not encouraging fathers to be authoritarian but this father's sudden show of personality had in this instance made an impression on his 16 year old daughter.

Family Time

—A 15 year old girl is going to a party and you know that there will be alcohol. This is a frightening situation. On many occasions you have mentioned the importance of handing over responsibility to the children but how do we handle a situation like that?

—When you fight for something and you meet resistance you need to consider whether you are fighting because you think you know what is best for the child or you are fighting for yourself—or perhaps both. If you won't let her go to the party because you are nervous and probably won't be able to sleep, then it is for your sake. A good piece of advice to parents in any difficult situation is this: *When nothing else works, try the truth.* Tell your daughter that she could consider staying at home for your sake. If she wants to go, then there is nothing else you can do but cross your fingers and hope she will be alright. The next morning you will know if it was a good party or not. Don't present her with interview style questions about it but if it looks like she didn't have a good night, you can acknowledge this and say: "It seems like you didn't have such a good night, is that right?" If she starts talking about what she didn't like, you can open a bottle of champagne in celebration. It is far more important to be able to keep the dialog open than to prevent the occasional bad night.

When nothing else works, try the truth.

Any parent of an alcoholic, drug addict or prostitute will always tell you to do your best to stay in contact. Keep the dialog open. If your son is an addict, it is alright to set limits if you are being abused—you can still keep the dialog open. Most parents go through a tremendous process of personal development when they have to deal with self-destructive children—once they get past the feeling of guilt, that is. When parents continually feel the need to check that their decisions and instruction have been followed, it is because they fear that the worst can happen.

Just like the childhood years, the teenage years can be likened to a marathon—the teenagers have to run it themselves. It is important not to run it for them—you shouldn't even run with them. You should however, be there as a safety net and make sure you are available. Whether or not it is possible to deal with a crisis together depends on the quality of the existing relationship and if the lines of communication are open. If you have challenged your 11 year old son's decision to buy a computer game you will know how well he considers things and what he thinks is important and what is not. When he reaches the age of 14 or 15 you will know when he is able to work things out by himself and when he needs some help. If you lecture him about what is a sensible thing to do and you are met with a strange look, then you might not be doing the right thing. Is he making sensible decisions or is he not?

The fact that we declare teenagers incapable of managing their own affairs is a reasonably new phenomenon. Not that long ago many children left home when they were just 10 years old. When you feel nervous and are worried about your teenager, it might be a good idea to try and remember how you felt at that age. I became a sailor when I was 15 years old. Some of my colleagues were 40 years or older and I was exposed to a world of temptations. There was unrestricted access to alcohol, drugs, fights and women. I worked 16 hours a day for a psychopath and with drunken colleagues. Did I survive? Yes! Did I learn anything? Yes, absolutely! It taught me to put things in perspective.

Allow me to share another example. I met a couple who had adopted a daughter. She was 15 years old when I spoke with them. The parents were deeply moral people and both teachers in a relatively small community. Their daughter went to a boarding school but wasn't happy there. It was an understatement to say that the mother was concerned. I told her what I thought and she gently replied: "Well, there is something you are not aware of, which I must tell you. Our daughter has a rare chromosomal disorder, which amongst other things, means that she is at risk of dying if she drinks alcohol. What you refer to as my being over-protective is in fact necessary for her survival." I asked the daughter to contribute to the conversation and share with us if she had drunk alcohol. It turned out that she had in fact been drunk on many occasions. The mother thought that her protection and warnings had a preventative effect but the reality was completely different. When parents are in a situation like that, they are the ones in need of help—not the children. They ought to sit down with their daughter and her friends and listen to them. Find out what they think, how they look after each other and if they have thought of any strategies should things go wrong. Say to them: "Please don't lie to me in an effort to reassure me. I would like to hear the truth." By doing this parents can put their minds at rest and at the same time do the girls a great favor. It is an important vote of confidence to ask teenagers for help.

—In other words; it is alright to agree that all the decisions are up to the teenagers. Of course parents should be ready with advice and follow-up but it is essentially up to the teenagers to sort things out.

—Yes! If I am dreaming of traveling the world during my gap-year, then it is my responsibility to do it. I cannot simply say that I want to do it and then count on my parents or the bank to finance the trip. Personal responsibility is first and foremost about taking responsibility for our own emotions; it is not about blaming someone else.

My son was very diplomatic. When he moved out of our home we hired a truck and I drove all his stuff to his new place. Then I thought: "What does a responsible father do now?" I didn't have a good role model myself because my father hardly ever said anything to me. From my son I had learned that I needed to ask whenever I wasn't sure how to go about being a father. So I asked him: "Would you like some good tips now?" He thought about this for a while and with a twinkle in his eye he said: "Yes, three good tips please!" This was very clever of him. Had he said that he didn't want any advice, I would have been sad and disappointed. Had he simply accepted my offer of advice, he would have had to listen to me for hours. Instead he solved it for both of us. Then I suddenly had to think very carefully about which were the three most important pieces of advice I could give him. This was difficult. Most parents feel they have plenty of advice to give their children but are not able to share it with them simply because their children don't want to listen to what they have to say. It is important to remember that if your children have reached puberty you shouldn't meddle in their personal lives unless you are invited to.

If your children have reached puberty you shouldn't meddle in their personal lives unless you are invited to.

—Can we talk about a teenager's bedroom? Do they have the right to privacy in there? To what extent is it our duty to keep it tidy? Do we need to knock before we go in? Do we check their phones and diaries?

—As a general rule, I believe the line is drawn at their door. From the ages of 11 or 12 I consider the child's private life to be exactly that—*private*. Of course you will need to knock, and you certainly shouldn't read their diaries or check their phones. This is common sense. But what do you do if you think something suspicious is going on. If you feel it is necessary to cross the line of decency to get that information then there is a much bigger problem at stake than the one you are busy searching for. Namely, the problem of not being able to ask your teenager directly: "We have a suspicion that . . . is happening in your life. Is that right?" The issue might be that you don't think he or she is telling you the truth.

Can you expect a teenager to tidy and clean their own room? Yes, you can. If it works, fine. If it is followed by hours of weekly power struggles without making a difference to the room then it wasn't such a good idea. What you can expect depends on what works. You can pick any of the thousands of options available to you—this doesn't matter. What you need to remember though, is that no 14 year old suffers from cleaning or tidying their room. That is not asking too much. The rest depends on the type of communication between you. The same applies to relationships between parents. Both can expect that sex is part of the relationship—but that is not the issue. The question is what you do if sex is not part of your relationship?

—Most parents struggle to define how much their teenagers should contribute at home. Some believe they need to have duties because it is a healthy part of life, while others believe they need duties because things need to be done.

—Sure, and there are parents for whom the word *duty* isn't part of their vocabulary. This really is due to the first anti-authoritarian generation. They protested against the family values they were brought up with, especially the fact that everything was about *obligations* and *conformity*. "No more duties!" they yelled and unfortunately everything then focused on what they would like to do instead. Doing only what we *want to do* symbolizes the democratic parents—a political freedom mantra. These parents will constantly ask their children what they would like to do. They feel it is an injustice to ask children to do something they don't want to. This is very unfortunate because teenagers understand the difference between *wants* and *needs*. If they are allowed to do whatever they want they will grow up believing that this is the way to live their lives. Reality however, is obviously different. Psychopaths are the ones who only do what they feel like doing. To live a quality life we must learn to formulate dreams and goals, and do our best to achieve these. Much of what we need to do to achieve those goals isn't necessarily pleasurable. It requires self-discipline and it's hard work. A life lived full of individual pleasures is a very anti-social life.

—Personal responsibility requires we are able to define our own dreams and goals?

—You are able to learn that things are your responsibility. Many parents mistakenly think that their teenagers are too busy with their school work, co-curricular activities and social lives to burden them with duties at home. While this might sound like a loving thought, it is not very appropriate. Any 12 or 13 year old is fully capable of taking responsibility for their own clothes, change when they need to, wash the clothes, hang them out to dry and iron. He or she can also shop and cook for themselves, tidy and clean their own rooms, and get to wherever they want to go. It is not a question of them having to do it all by themselves but if they need help, it is their responsibility to ask for it. They shouldn't take for granted any service provided to them. If nobody is able to cook for them they must do it themselves. If teenagers were able and allowed to handle more things by themselves, much of their parents' frustration would disappear.

Parents shouldn't expect their teenagers to do these things willingly and with the greatest of pleasure, as they will most likely think they have more important things to do. They might be angry and dissatisfied but that doesn't mean you are asking too much of them. Don't think that you do them any favors by giving them an *out of duty pass*. If a ship has four crew members—then all four of them must sail the ship. As part of a community it is, in fact, important to contribute, otherwise you will very quickly lose your dignity.

Any 12 or 13 year old is fully capable of taking responsibility for their own clothes, change when they need to, wash the clothes, hang them out to dry and iron. He or she can also shop and cook for themselves, tidy and clean their own rooms, and get to wherever they want to go.

You must be prepared to re-negotiate everyone's duties now and again. This is also what happens in any workplace—you must be flexible. It is not a good idea to moralize: "You really shouldn't do things that way!" If your home has become a hotel for your teenager then you can say: "We have been operating a hotel. We realize that this was wrong so we are going to stop doing that. If you would like to live here with us, you will have to do some of the duties as part of this community." If you want to do your teenagers a favor then you will ask them to pull their weight. It must concern something that needs to be done—not just a duty for the sake of it. As a parent you can choose if you would like *helpful* children or *conscientious* ones.

When my son lived with us I cooked dinner every day. Every now and then I had a few minutes break so I would set the table. It wouldn't be fair to call my son and demand that he set the table. That would be a duty just for the sake of it. If however, I needed help, I asked him. As parents we have to be very careful not to mix love and business by requesting proof of their love for us. "We have loved you for 12 years. Now you have the opportunity to help and to prove that you also love us." Using this as the reason why they should help would not be fair. You wouldn't say something along those lines to another adult either.

—A little while ago I read some research into sick-leave in the workforce. The research found that the generation whose homes were like hotels ended up spending a substantial amount of time away from work.

—The industrial society's draconian requirements and duties are slowly making room also for our personal needs. There are obviously those who are still not able to understand that the employer and employee have shared needs. This is indeed why we at FamilyLab have an increased focus on working with organizations.

People are no longer so worried about what the community might think. Since the 1980s, more and more children have grown up with greater feelings of self-worth. We notice that these children have a strong sense of social responsibility, which brings us back to the relationship and the question about what constitutes a good relationship? Above all, it is a relationship which allows both parties to take responsibility for themselves and their emotions and boundaries. We know that if the relationship is based on *servicing* each other then it will fail. Just as things will go seriously wrong if we raise our children based on *stimulation* and *entertainment*.

—A 15 year old girl has a boyfriend who is the sort of boy her parents were hoping she would never meet. He is unpleasant and stands for everything the family doesn't like—yet the daughter has fallen for him. What do the parents do?

—They say to their daughter: "We are in a dilemma and really need your help. We can't hide that we would prefer if you break up with him, but we realize that this is not going to happen. How can we find a solution?" Their daughter will most likely claim that they would think differently if they knew him. Then the parents could say: "Alright, would it be okay with you if we invite him over so we can talk to him about that?" If the parents want access to her private life they need permission. If they are granted permission they could say to her partner: "We have invited you because we have a problem. Our daughter is very much in love with you and you with her. Yet, we aren't so keen on you. What can we do? Would it be alright if we asked you a few questions?" The parents have laid the foundation for a good relationship with the young man—or for the daughter to see him in a different light. Based on more nuanced information the daughter will inevitably consider if she wants to continue the relationship. This is a direct method that requires decency, politeness and responsibility. The parents assume responsibility for their own dilemmas. It is not up to the daughter to resolve these.

> *Far too many pearls of wisdom are never picked up by teenagers simply because we didn't ask whether they wanted them or not. Love without honesty and timing doesn't work.*

—Your opinion is that the fundamental platform must be dialog all the way through?

—When children reach their teenage years we shouldn't approach them with questions and good advice without being invited. This means you can say: "There is something important I would like to talk to you about, can you let me now when it suits you?" Far too many pearls of wisdom are never picked up by teenagers simply because we didn't ask whether they wanted them or not. Love without honesty and timing doesn't work.

—What can we do to support a teenager's feeling of self-worth?

—It is most important that they feel they matter and are valued by you as their parents. This doesn't just mean they need to be good at school or have some good friends. It means they need to feel: "My mother's quality of life has improved because she has been with me for the past 14 years."

When your teenager is on the journey of becoming more independent (a few years before they move out) you could think about how he or she has enriched your life. Maybe you give a little speech at their confirmation, or write a song, a poem or put together a little book—something that you can give them. To visualize and draw attention to their value to you as parents is a very precious gift. Worries and limitations only serve as a way for the parents to feel important. This won't give teenagers more self-esteem or a greater feeling of self-worth.

—What happens to teenagers' feelings of self-worth when they assume responsibility for their own actions?

—The feeling of self-worth is by far the best defense against everything and anything parents might worry about. From education to sex, drugs and rock 'n roll. Self-worth is the most precious gift you can ever give them—and they happily give plenty of it in return. This is one of the essential ingredients of raising children, namely that it is not solely something parents give to children. The very best way to help them build their feeling of self-worth is trust, trust and more trust. This doesn't mean you can trust that they will do what you stand for but that they will make the best possible decisions based on their personal experiences. Naturally, it follows that they will also make wrong decisions.

The very best way to help them build their feeling of self-worth is trust, trust and more

> *trust. This doesn't mean you can trust that they will do what you stand for but that they will make the best possible decisions based on their personal experiences.*

During the teenage years, parents' worries and concerns will be unwelcome intruders into the family. This has a seriously negative effect on their feelings of self-worth. Worries are an expression of mistrust. When we at FamilyLab speak with teenagers, they have a whole spectrum of questions but two issues run like a red thread through them all. "How can I live my life so that I am able to retain my integrity, my values and my dreams—without making my parents sad or worry too much?" This is a very sophisticated question. Just a generation ago this wasn't the issue. Then it was more like: "How can I live my life without my parents finding out what I do?" That generation lived part of their lives hidden from their parents. This is not so today, which is challenging for parents, because there are so many things to relate to and decisions to make. You have no autopilot to rely on. Nevertheless, it is as challenging as it is rewarding. It is indeed exciting and even more so because parents and teenagers have never before had so many deep and meaningful conversations as they have these days. Many parents are, without doubt, envious and would give anything to have had a similar rapport with their own parents.

Research has taught us much about infants and babies. Since the 1970s we have, through modern psychotherapy, also gained a more in-depth understanding of what it means to be an adult—especially thanks to the *women's liberation movement* and the demands for *equal opportunities* that followed. However, two age groups have been left out completely: young people and seniors. Our ways of dealing with these two groups have, by and large, remained unchanged and are as primitive as they were about a hundred years ago.

Everywhere around the world people are talking about the so-called *impossible youths* but you really don't need to be an expert to know that when a couple of gangs attack each other they do it for two underlying reasons:

1. Because they don't feel valued by their parents or by society.
2. Because of their own personal anxieties.

If a so-called *well-functioning* 18 year old went to see a psychologist and said he suffered from anxiety he would receive plenty of care. However, if he stood on a street corner looking angry and aggressive, and was dressed in dirty jeans and leather, he would be met with suspicion and aggression. This is the grotesque and tragic reality.

It is no good trying to find solutions to these issues by applying more of the same. Typically parents and school will get together and agree to stand together, set clear boundaries, and so forth. Sure, this will make the adults feel good but it won't work because they won't get together afterwards to discuss why things didn't work. They won't get together simply because they will see it as personal failure. The real and necessary challenge for parents is to enter into an honest dialog with each other. If they are not able to communicate with each other, then learning this skill is what is needed first and foremost. It will benefit them at this point in time and when their children have moved out.

—*What are the most common challenges for boys and girls during their teenage years?*

—It is not possible to answer that question because they develop so quickly and teenagers meet new challenges all the time. I can however, give you an example: A father lived on his own with his son for around eight or nine years. Today the boy is 17 and studying. They have always had a good relationship until the son made new friends and one day he sat in their home smoking hash. The father rang me and asked what he should do. I told him not to challenge his son—instead he should challenge himself by asking these three questions:

1. "Where are my limits?"
2. "What can I accept?"
3. "What am I not prepared to accept?"

He thought about that for a few weeks. Then he rang and told me his original question was no longer relevant. When you find answers to those three questions there is no need to ask anyone else. He said to his son: "Listen, I don't want this in my home. If you want to live like that you will have to find somewhere else to live!" That was all he said. No fuss and no scary stories about what could possibly happen—just a clear message. Three days later the son said: "I have decided that I do want to live here." Then he stopped smoking hash.

Parents need to focus on their own personal limits instead of focusing on their doubts, threats, criticism or questions. When parents seek professional help it is very often the child they talk about and not themselves. They are not fully aware of who they are themselves and thus they rarely get proper help.

Parents must take responsibility for themselves before they can become role models for responsible children.

Many parents with teenagers have some gruesome memories of their own youth. They remember how they themselves behaved and the things that happened to them. I remember a party that ended with friends being sick, people turning up who weren't invited, and so forth. We ended up spending the rest of the night cleaning up broken glass and rubbish. We tried to remove all evidence of the party. We were scared our parents would find out. What is the moral here? We had lots of secrets and I think we were extremely lucky nothing much went wrong.

—*I was reasonably good at school in general but I do remember my fear of those comments in red. I just wanted my grade because the red comments would highlight my imperfections. I was good at Math but my teacher would continually focus on my mistakes. This lead to a performance anxiety and I left school with unsatisfactory Math results—and good grades in every other subject. Today, when I try to help my children with their Math homework I suffer anxiety attacks. I get angry and push the books away.*

—That is a very typical and common example. Things go completely wrong when parents try to do what their childhood teachers did. Children are born with an ability to learn everything they have to learn. Ideally, your Math teacher would have said: "What is happening with you and your Math, Monica? What is it you find difficult? How can I help you?" Everybody knows that teaching ought to be targeted at the individual. Nevertheless, schools find it difficult to implement. Some schools only know right or wrong. Your Math teacher most likely thought he helped you by drawing attention to what you got wrong—so you could improve. In brief, this is what happens in the brain: a number of the synapses that amongst other things deal with mathematics connect with the brain stem (the most primitive part of our brain). When you have to deal with mathematics you become anxious, and anxiety is a very basic reaction in the brain stem. This is what happens to you. Are you able to change the way you react? Sure, the brain is the only organ which is elastic and develops throughout our lives while other organs diminish. When you alter your behavior you also alter your mind.

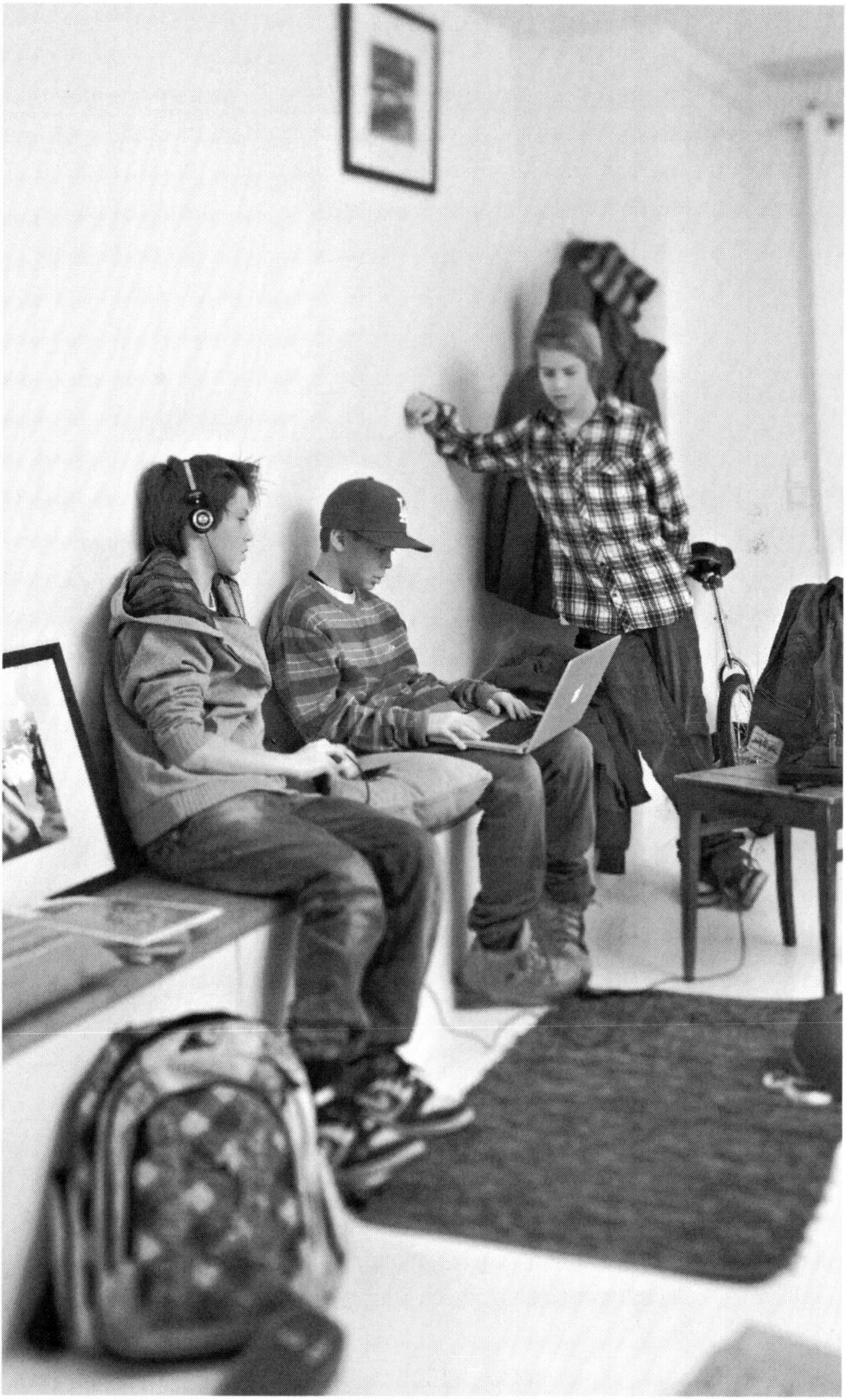

Many people react in very primitive ways—for example when they separate and divorce. According to recent brain research this is because of very early *separation anxieties* that were traumatic experiences or it might be due to experiences of unexpected and unforeseen abuse. The brain consists of connections and is shaped by the human relationships we belong to. Inside your brain the circumstances surrounding your learning influence your abilities to learn. If people around you criticize you and focus on your mistakes then any learning will be difficult. Your mathematic abilities have been restricted because of the atmosphere your teacher created.

When I studied to become a teacher there were discussions questioning whether or not students should be graded for the work they did. I don't believe this is the most important question regarding students and their learning. We need to stop thinking that people will thrive as long as they are praised. Praise releases endorphins in the brain (a feeling of happiness) but this is short lived and can become addictive. I have written much about the subject of praise and received many letters from readers. A 15 year old Norwegian girl wrote to me and expressed very clearly what this is all about:

"I am a 15 year old girl and throughout my childhood I have always been praised by both friends and family. During the past three years I have spent a lot of time playing sport, dancing and doing my homework. As a result I have received plenty of positive feedback and good comments. I was also given top grades in just about every subject at school. It is my impression that I top my class. After every dance lesson my instructor says to me: "Wonderful work, you're outstanding!" At sport my coach always tells me that I am the best player on the field.

In the beginning it was wonderful to be praised and acknowledged. I was extremely happy. But after a while I didn't want to leave the dance lessons without a word of praise from my instructor. I depended on it! If I didn't receive top grades or put in a top performance I was devastated—I was destroyed. A couple of years ago I actually thought that I could be best at everything I did. As a result I became very competitive and had to do and achieve everything. I wore myself out completely.

The sad thing is that all the encouraging comments I get hardly mean anything to me anymore. I just cannot get enough positive feedback from people around me and I have lost the ability to enjoy what I am doing. I have become a slave to what other people think of me. I have also had enough of feeling that I always have to be the best and continually compare myself to others—especially the other girls at dancing. The competition between us is immense. I feel like giving up but that is almost impossible. Life is very difficult for me and I feel I need help."

—That is a very touching letter—I can recognize myself. How did you respond to her?

—I wrote:

"Your letter describes your situation very clearly. It is the most personal letter of all the ones I have received from both adults and young people. Each of these people tell me their personal stories explaining how too much praise leaves a devastating inner emptiness. You have been able to express this better than any of them. This, in fact, makes me rather sad because now I know how many other young people are struggling with similar existential issues. Many of these young people see doctors who incorrectly diagnose them as being depressive and prescribe "happy pills". Other young people develop eating disorders or begin to self-harm. It is saddening that so many doctors are unable to differentiate between *emotional problems and existential crises. The health system is full of old-fashioned attitudes and lacks knowledge—especially when it comes to children and young people. This makes your letter an invaluable document that hopefully will be able to support others who are not able to reflect and express themselves with the same profound insight as you.*

I agree with you: you do need some help. I hope that you with the help of your parents or your school, will be able to see a psychologist or therapist. One who understands the damage praise can do and who is willing to spend a year or more helping you find yourself again. I do not think you need to worry about what your subconscious might reveal. You have not been abused or exposed to serious neglect. Your "dependence" or "addiction" is praise, and you do not need it to soothe pain, anxiety or confusion. It feels good to be praised but you have a strong enough feeling of self-worth to say stop and evaluate the way you are living. Part of this ability is due to your parents, and I hope they will be able to help find new and healthier ways of loving and supporting you in the years to come. If not, I am confident that you are able to do it by yourself with the support from good friends and others who respect you regardless of your achievements. Consider carefully who you think will be true friends!

It is my experience that it might be difficult for you to find a professional with whom you can work really well. Remember that it is alright to be selective and you do not have to waste your time with someone who only wants to focus on your self-confidence. Ironically, I actually did rather well at school and sport but it was never acknowledged and I did not feel recognized. For years I went through some serious soul-searching and saw several psychotherapists who all said: "You need to learn to receive praise!" They all said the same thing. (All of them, just like me, belong to a generation which relied on criticism and very little praise.) I was torn between my own experiences and my respect for their authority. Every time I was praised I became sad—and they thought I ought to be happy! It took years before I realized that the therapists were wrong. Every time I was praised I connected with my deep-seated desire to be seen and to be recognized. This sadness was a stark reminder of the sadness I had previously experienced for those very same reasons. Nevertheless, I myself made similar mistakes as a therapist until I was taken to task by a young and very beautiful woman. She had been my client for a few months and one day she said: "Jesper, if you really cannot understand that it is possible to be beautiful and at the same time feel like shit then I have to find another therapist. All my life I have been looked at—now I want to be seen!" She knew, much better than I did, that this is often the problem for beautiful, smart and clever people. They are looked at, admired, flattered and praised but rarely seen as the unique human beings they also are.

You are lucky because you have already worked out that something isn't working. Perhaps you need to take a break from your dancing and sport? Then again, you activities are not your real problem. The problem is (was!) the way you relate to them and your unrealistic expectations to how they could enrich your life—make you happy. A granddad asked his five year old grandchild: "What do you want to be when you grow up?" He answered: "The best!" So the granddad asked: "The best what?" To which the boy answers: "The best at being me, of course!"

I wish you all the best of luck with your journey of discovery and look forward to hearing more about what you learn along the way."

—That girl had the advantage of being able to express herself. How is she going now?

—She is seeing a psychologist and she has brought her parents along a few times. They were understanding enough to agree that she should stop dancing if she was doing it for the wrong reasons. I know other parents who don't accept it when their children want to end careers otherwise destined for stardom. I met a woman some years ago who had won a number of Olympic medals but it never made much difference to her whether she won or lost. The media didn't get it. They didn't understand why she didn't break down when she didn't win a gold medal. She simply smiled and thought everything was just fine. At the opposite end of the spectrum we know the tennis star Goran Ivanišević who won Wimbledon as a wild card. He didn't have a healthy sense of self-worth and sometimes threw tantrums when the umpire's decision didn't go his way. He became very angry, swore and protested profusely. If, on the other hand, he won, everything would be fine. The Danish Anja Andersen who is an European handball player grew up with praise, praise and more praise for just one thing, namely her ability to play European handball. Her father also played. She was a lovely girl and very sociable when her team had won a number of games but the instant she didn't play so well, she would behave like a two year old.

A child who tries to achieve perfection at school will not take his time to find answers to questions. He gives up, gets angry and unhappy. Then he will try to guess the answer because he thinks he ought to know straight away. Not only does he want to perform all the time he also wants to be perfect.

I am not trying to criticize parents who praise a lot but I do want to draw attention to the fact that it has the opposite effect. A child who tries to achieve perfection at school will not take the time to find answers to questions. He gives up, gets angry and unhappy. Then he will try to guess the answer because he thinks he ought to know straight away. Not only does he want to perform all the time, he also wants to be perfect. He doesn't feel he can live without perfection. His parents need to acknowledge that they did what they thought was best for him but now they realize that all the praise installed a *fear of failure* in him.

Those "experts" who specialize in children's behavior will often advocate the carrot/stick method: if you understand what I want you to understand you will be praised—but if you don't understand you will be punished. The experts don't like me when I say this is an outdated psychology. In a sense they are right because children will do the right things when they are praised and/or punished. What they are not able to do is develop their feeling of self-worth. The carrot/stick method does not respect children and ignores who they are—they are not seen or recognized. Those children will do anything—whatever it takes—to be praised. As adults they will live through hell. When they start work they will realize that no employer will praise them 24/7. Then they lose the fixed point in their lives and internalize things. Yet, they will find nothing—unless they find pain and suffering which they are not able to manage.

Imagine you are at a gallery opening and a good friend of yours is exhibiting his paintings. He asks what you think and you answer: "Well . . . You are improving the way you use the warm colors." That is praise. Deep down you know that your friend really wants to know if his painting means something to you, and if so, what? When you talk to him about that, you give him a personal response which is what we as humans need.

There is a difference between being really pleased about something and boasting about it.

People who have a well developed sense of self-worth are not concerned with praise. If I think I am good only when others tell me so then something is completely wrong. That is what ultimately happens to many of those youths who are continually praised by their parents and teachers. To them, all this praise is proof they are talented so they come to believe they are absolutely fantastic. Then they start a career and get a job which lasts all of three weeks. They will be shell-shocked. There is nothing wrong with being good, nice or a world champion sprinter or chess player. That is wonderful but things go seriously wrong when we start believing that this is what life is all about. There are plenty of examples of superstars in the areas of sport, culture, acting or the finance world who live an illusion. Suddenly, they face emptiness and are thrown into a terrible personal crisis. This easily leads to depression and drug abuse. Parents must stop pumping up their children's egos. In many families the children walk around with such big egos that it makes them sick. Clinically speaking this is called: *inflated ego*. We all know how unpleasant it is to be with someone whose ego is inflated and always needs attention. I once had such a friend. He bought a very big house and just couldn't stop bragging about it. I visited him with a good American colleague who was asked what he thought of the house. He answered: "It seems like there is nothing left for me to think. You already think everything!" He was spot on. There is a difference between being really pleased about something and boasting about it. When you express how pleased you are with something then there is plenty of room for other people's opinions too.

—A child's feeling of self-worth changes when parents and teachers use personal feedback instead of praise?

—Many things happen when children are given *personal feedback*. You are right, their feeling of self-worth grows in a way that cannot happen when they are praised. When adults start searching for children's personal reactions their feelings of self-worth will also grow. They get a better understanding of self and become better at using their personal language. This is a classic example of the fact that raising children works best when it is a mutual and reciprocal process. The same actually happens in our relationships. When we stop saying "I" and instead say "you" we will start arguing. When it comes to interacting with children we tend to use "you" far too often!!

> *When adults start searching for children's personal reactions their feelings of self-worth will also grow. They get a better understanding of self and become better at using their personal language. This is a classic example of the fact that raising children works best when it is a mutual and reciprocal process.*

—*By modifying our language we will be able to teach our children without lecturing to them? Will it improve the learning of students if we are able to stop using our "power of definition"?*

—The Norwegian researcher and Associate Professor at Oslo University College, Dr Berit Bae has researched *recognition* as part of pedagogical relationships. She uses the term: *The adult's power to define*. I believe that this power to define and verbally or mentally label children is crucial when we try to understand why relationships between people so often fail. Adults are very concerned about bullying amongst children. Then they realized that adults also bully and that bullying happens everywhere. *The power to define* is bullying simply by verbally or mentally labeling a child as dumb, impolite, silly, childish or whatever. It really shouldn't surprise us that children bully if they have grown up with parents and teachers who constantly use their *power to define* who they are. The fact that adults use their *power to define* is probably the single most damaging way we harm our children and our relationship with them. This also applies to many relationships between adults.

This is the reason why it is so important that we develop *our personal language*. The language where we describe and express ourselves instead of defining others. Some other alternatives have been proposed and are called: *non-violent communication*. Personal language creates good, honest and strong relationships. Defining language only destroys relationships and creates nothing but winners and losers.

—*What is our motivation for using this power to define?*

—Well, when you use it, you realize that it gives you power—and we can become addicted to power. It doesn't do much good spending millions of dollars on anti-bullying programs. They do help—but only briefly. I have come across an interesting case study, which I would like to share with you. I once worked with a family that had communication problems. The father was an officer in the army. His wife and four daughters did not like him. They were unhappy about just about everything and the poor man didn't know what to do. He was a responsible man, very intelligent and had attended numerous communication seminars. Nevertheless, he didn't understand what I said to him, even though he really wanted to. During the summer break we stopped therapy for a while and when he returned he was very pleased. He said to me: "Jesper, I think I get it now!" He had been renovating his garage and needed to borrow a drill from his brother. Every time he rang his brother the line was engaged. In his language the tone of the engaged phone sounded like: "you-you-you-you-you . . ." He suddenly realized that the five ladies in his life constantly got the engaged tone when they wanted to speak with him. They couldn't contact him because the only way he was able to express himself was by saying: "you-you-you..!" He paid greater attention to *what* he needed to say than to *how* he said it. Perhaps a bit like many other men and school teachers. When he said: "You are like *this* or you should do *that*..!" then he felt certain that it was the right way. "Maybe it is the right way..?" I said to him. "But that is not what is most important. The question is whether you *want* to make contact with people? Do you want a dialog or do you want to be a lonely leader who always knows what is right?

The feeling of freedom, the desire to let go and to accept love without strict conditions and expectations . . . It sounds so nice in theory. This is what most of us hope for in our relationships. It does feel as if we can achieve this—at least for a little while. Then reality kicks in and we begin to blame our partner because we have lost our freedom, identity and enthusiasm. Eventually, separation might be the solution. Although this might also be an escape from what we need to learn about ourselves and our interactions with other people. Nevertheless, for some, separation is the only way out.

—*I would like to talk about teenagers whose parents have separated. When the children are old enough they will most likely prefer one home to the other.*

—If the parents are able to treat each other decently (the same way they treat strangers) then the children will be brave enough to ask if they can move to live with the mother or the father. The children are free to choose what is best for them at the time. The important thing is for the parent they ask to answers: "Of course you can!" The more conflicts there are between the parents the more difficult it will be to work out why the children want to move. What are their motives?

Often the accusations start flowing back and forth: "She just wants to live with her father because he doesn't set any limits but I do!" An eight year old would very rarely make such superficial decisions. Why does the eight year old want to live with her father? Perhaps she wants to look after him because her mother has found a new partner. In that case it is most likely because eight years ago the mother decided to have a child with a man who mentally was like a six year old. It is not good when the daughter feels she needs to care for her father.

Many parents who consult FamilyLab when they consider separating immediately start talking about what is best for the child. However, this is the wrong place to start. We must start talking about what is best for the parents. Perhaps both will say: "I would like the child to live with me!" Once they get this out of their system and put their arguments forward they become more flexible. If instead they keep it bottled up inside and use it as a secret agenda by including it in a polite and sensible conversation then they will end up with a compromise which doesn't satisfy anyone.

A 16 year old girl once wrote to me on behalf of her friend who was two years older. The friend's parents had what everyone thought was a happy marriage. One day, out of the blue, the father left. He had met someone else. The parents tried therapy and mediation. They couldn't talk to each other. They tried to write and meet, it just didn't work. The daughter became more and more unhappy by being used as a piece in their board game. The girl who wrote to me wondered how her unhappy friend could set some boundaries for herself. That was exactly what she had to do.

—Sure, but what do you say to a girl when you feel that her parents are putting each other down—even though they know that the child will spend time with the other?

—You offer the child all the care and comfort you muster—and encourage the parents to grow up, quickly!

—*When I was young a lot of parents separated. My friends were very open and honest about the situation at home. We spoke about which parent they could trust. Are you able to say something about trust to parents in the case of separation—how can the parents build trust?*

—Trust is only built when parents behave decently and have a decent relationship with each other—and do not slander each other. They must tell their children the truth about their separation, listen to the children and take their feelings and wishes seriously. If they don't, then the separation will most likely become highly traumatizing for everyone involved—children as well as adults.

A girl expressed it like this: "My parents just moved away from each other. It was I who separated." That was a profound observation. Fortunately, it is possible to experience a separation differently. I know families who continue to be families after the separation. They go on holidays together, celebrate birthdays together—and the new partners are part of this. Some think this is wrong but the reality is that people do the best they can when they are together and many are also capable of doing it when they are no longer together. There is no point in telling them that they should do it for the children's sake. If they were able to sacrifice themselves for their children then they would not separate in the first place.

—*What can you do if the rules are different in the two different homes? Let's say that the father doesn't allow the teenage son to drink alcohol but the mother does.*

—Then he is presented with a unique opportunity to work out what he wants. Deep down, the desire to synchronize rules and values is all about the parents' need for power and control or mistrust and fear. It is impossible to gain power and control over a teenager. Mistrust and fear are emotions that belong to the parents. They have to take responsibility for this instead of passing the burden onto their children.

—*Does one parent have the right to decide what happens at the other parents' place?*

—No, not at all! The moment you separate from another person you lose every right to interfere with what happens in that person's personal life.

> *The moment you separate from another person you lose every right to interfere with what happens in that person's personal life.*

—*What makes you say this with such conviction?*

—Because involvement requires love, trust and care. This is exactly what has gone—but if it is possible, then that is wonderful.

The idea that the same rules and conditions must exist at both places is absurd. Then you would be saying that rules are the most important part of the child's life and development. This is obviously not so. Most important are the people with whom the child lives. It is not even alright to force parents to live near each other after a separation. Then the child would have to shoulder the responsibility for the father not being able to take the job he has always wanted because it is in another city, or for the mother not being able to live with her new partner because his home is further away. The child would have to shoulder a burden that is far too heavy. And after around 15 years the mother will be crying because of lost love.

—But how do you deal with the criticism from an ex if you go your own way and do what you think is best—even though it is contrary to what the ex believes in?

—You will have to define your own boundaries as clearly as possible. "I might need some parental advice but I won't ask you!" If you are the one criticizing, you must remember that every time you criticize your child's mother or father you are creating very unfortunate conditions for your child. Regardless of whether the parents live together or not, any power struggle between them is about the child who will either feel guilty and/or be forced to take sides.

—So the traditional idea about doing things exactly the same way at both places is not good?

—I believe this was something parents did to reduce their personal feelings of guilt. Face it: there are two families—it is no longer just one. This is the way to allow the children to deal with their frustrations, pain and loss.

—It cannot be easy for children to confront their parents when they think differently about things such as eating habits, personal responsibility, and so forth. They will quickly start to identify with one of the parents.

—Sure, this is often the price children have to pay. We might wish that things were different but this is the way it is. The children need support—not two parents who continue to argue. It is never easy to confront your parents but children have to learn this in order to grow up and develop into healthy adults.

Boys from 16 to 18 years old might find it particularly difficult to confront their mothers. But they will have to break away from her so they can grow up and form their own relationships. As a mother you can teach them that it is perfectly alright to say: "No!" Say to them: "It is much worse if you lie than if you say "No!" to me" One of the benefits of separation is that children learn that more than one truth exists. It is a way for them to connect with their own voice and it will enable them to make decisions independently. Being able to say: "No!" is very important. It is actually easier to do when we realize that there is more than one truth. When two parents have different opinions it is possible for children to form their own opinions—and be brave enough to contradict their parents.

Until I met my wife she was not allowed to speak her mind. Nobody was interested in what she wanted. Then we met and I was interested in knowing what she had to say. You have to invite all sides of the truth into the relationship without condemning it—or the one speaking. Otherwise we lose our personal integrity. It might be easier skipping the truth or parts of it because we avoid the repercussions and the consequences. If we run away from the truth we avoid the pain but it is obviously a short-lived escape. Lying is ultimately more painful for the one lying than it is for the one who is being lied to.

Previous generations only had a moralistic attitude to truth: "It is wrong to lie. It makes your mother very sad and your father very angry!" This breaks down trust and limits the opportunities for an open conversation. It does not leave room for a dialog where both parties are able to learn more about each other. There is only one reason why children and young people lie: They sense that their parents cannot handle the truth. The child thinks like this: "My family cannot handle the truth about my behavior. They get too angry and too sad. A crisis between us inevitably follows. I better lie to avoid this."

When children and young people constantly lie, it is often part of a bigger problem. Those lying are trying to say: "I don't feel like a member of this family any longer and I don't care about their rules." Such a powerful reaction from a child is always based on a painful past. Most families will need professional help to unravel this.

There is only one reason why children and young people lie: They sense that their parents cannot handle the truth.

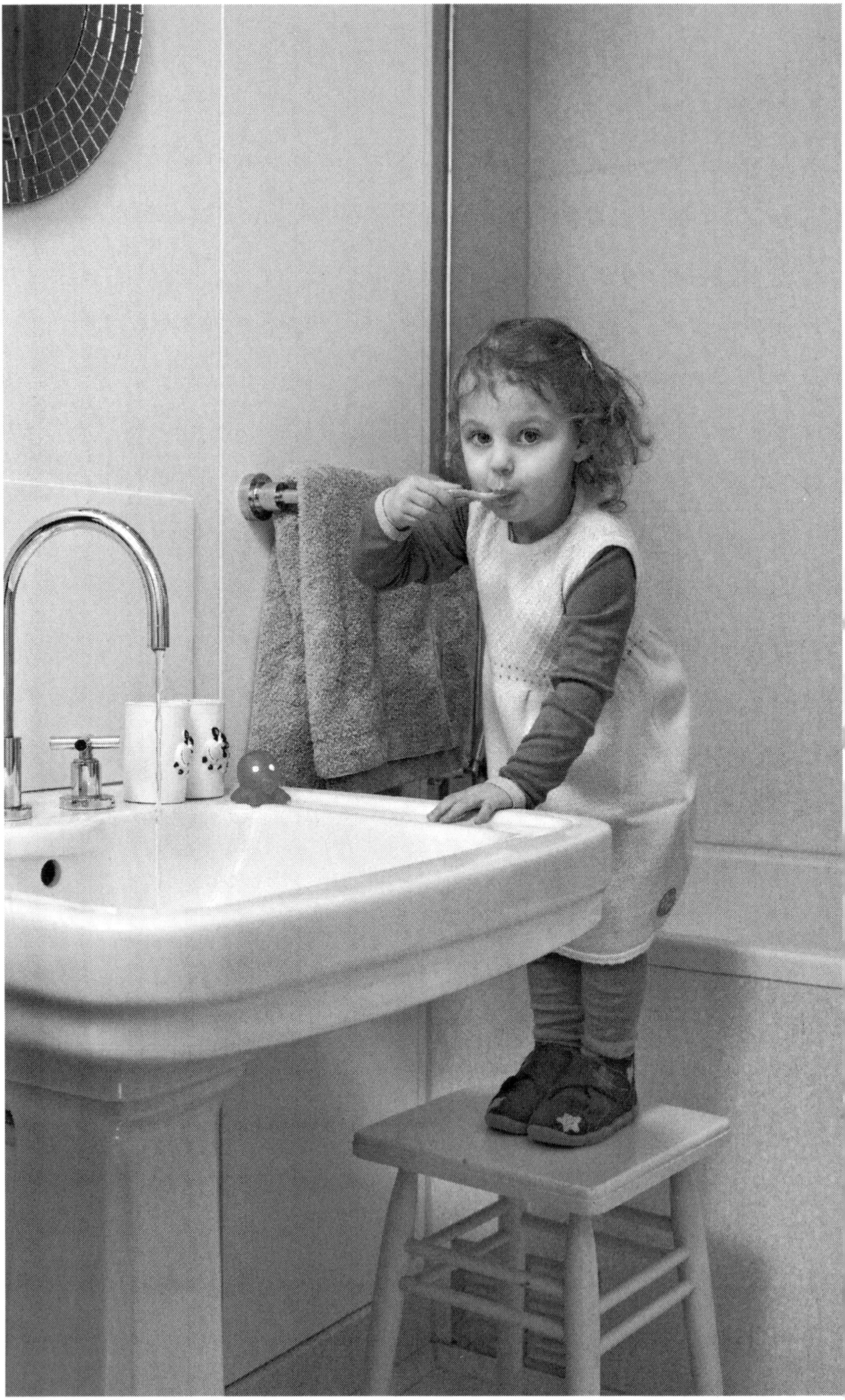

THE BATHROOM
– Body and hygiene

There is nothing as wonderful as a carefree child, one who doesn't have a worry in the world. One who is present right here and right now. One who lives and enjoys the moment. We are born naked but the natural comfort of being naked fades as we grow. We become conscious of our genitals, our figure and our gender, and soon we become shy and perhaps embarrassed. From the age of nine children become more and more ashamed of being naked. During puberty it obviously becomes important to understand and respect children's private areas. This is a period of time full of thoughts and feelings related to body, looks and belonging.

MONICA:
—*Chaos in the bathroom, rush-rush, tripping at the door, get out of the shower, where is the towel? Mornings can be stressful and chaotic. Who decides what happens and when it happens?*

JESPER:

—This is a great opportunity to start practicing *self-responsibility*. A number of pedagogical and parenting tips are popular these days—many of them aren't very good at all. One of these is to agree with the children at night what they are going to wear the next day. Most parents soon find out how unrealistic that is when dressing small children. Their ability to plan doesn't reach far—certainly not as far as the next day. If you feel conflicts are developing it is probably a good time to say: "I have been deciding what you were wearing. I sense you don't like that so I won't do that any longer. From now on you will take responsibility for what you wear and I can help you if you like." Then you will have to accept that they will make decisions you might not agree with. They might dress according to their mood and not the weather. Put it down to inexperience and let them learn from that. If you start complaining or try to change their mind things will go wrong. You could just say: "If you would like to know what I think then I think it is the wrong decision because it is cold outside. I would like to suggest that you find something else to wear." If it is winter and your child insists on wearing a summer dress to childcare then you need to be responsible and say: "That's fine, I'll just put some warm clothes in a bag and if you need it, you know where it is." By doing that, she will learn from her own mistakes. It is really simple and I have not yet met a family where the conflicts didn't stop shortly after this practice was introduced. It is a shift in our thinking. It might also require a bit of background explanation when you arrive at childcare. An alternative, which is less effective, would be to give the child a couple of options you have thought of beforehand. When your child doesn't want you to decide it doesn't mean that you should leave them completely alone. It is important that you are there as a support.

—*It does sound a bit dramatic..! Does this also apply to a child who is only two years old?*

—At two years of age children begin to develop their independence. Children do not learn much from being taught. They explore. That is why they will become highly frustrated when they are lectured to and when they are being dressed in clothes they don't want to wear. The aim is for them to help themselves to a greater and greater extent. It is always the parents who start the power struggle about clothes—mostly because they are in a hurry. If the child is not allowed to experiment, practice and fail then you take away the foundation for their self-confidence and feelings of self-worth. You will also turn the child into a helpless being by continually pointing out that you as a parent know better.

> *"Worry" is what kills a child's self-esteem. It is a declaration of mistrust.*

—*It is a given that today's children wear expensive brand labels. How can parents deal with that kind of pressure?*

—This is not an issue about *what* you do but *why* you do it. Most parents will choose *the road of least resistance*. They cannot cope with the conflicts. Many have tried moralizing and lecturing against social pressures but this very quickly becomes untrustworthy. Most parents are themselves equally preoccupied with body weight and dressing nicely. My parents were poor—in a western sense. When they eventually bought us new shoes they bought the best brand in the hope that they would last. In those days it was Adidas. Back then this was also a brand label so nothing much has changed. Children and young people have always compared themselves to each other. We have to find some values we can believe in. Some parents don't take their children shopping either because they don't want the children to see what they buy or because they don't think the children are able to choose wisely or they fear the children will want everything in the shop. It doesn't make sense to tell children that they have to make do with less when we ourselves are excessive consumers.

There are great differences between cultures. The Norwegian people become a little embarrassed and feel guilty when they buy really expensive things. In Croatia, the more expensive things are the prouder they feel. Some call this *status symbols* but that is nothing new. In the old days people formed tribes and dressed like everyone else or according to their status within the tribe. These days we are not part of a particular tribe if we cannot afford the clothes they wear. Parents are able to set an example and show their children what it means to have *personal integrity*. When an 11 year old girl has *personal integrity* she will do fine no matter what kind of clothes she wears. We worry about how our children will cope but *worry* is what kills their self-esteem. It is a declaration of mistrust.

Becoming a parent is full of paradoxes. Alongside a feeling of genuine love comes the feeling of worry. As parents we worry about everything from small daily things to the big challenges our children will have to face. We worry about how they are coping, how they develop and whether or not they are happy about themselves, their body and their looks.

—*You talk a great deal about personal responsibility. If you notice that your daughter spends a lot of time on the bathroom scales thinking she is overweight, how would you encourage her to adapt a healthier lifestyle without adding fuel to the problem?*

—Obesity is partly a genetic condition. An 11 year old might be self-conscious or be teased about her weight but that doesn't necessarily mean she is motivated to go on a diet. Were she to lose weight permanently she must want to do it for her own sake. I am not suggesting that parents should just sit back and wait. They could say: "We believe it is a problem because you think it is. We need your help to find out if you want to lose weight—and why? We also need to know what we can do to help you." Losing weight is like breaking an addiction and it is a very lonely journey. If your daughter finds it difficult walking past the fridge it will not make a big difference if you try to stop her. It is very important not to turn the extra kilos into the whole problem.

—What happens if a girl feels overweight but in reality is quite slender? As a parent, what can you do?

—Let us assume that this diagnosis is right and it is a question of unreasonable self-criticism. Then I am not sure there is in fact anything we can do. You can establish that her weight is normal and tell her not to worry about it. Most likely however, she will not listen to what her parents say anyway—it goes in one ear and out the other. In my experience this is one of those situations where the best thing you can do is to state the facts and then leave it. Wait for the girl to realize this herself. Then she will begin to regulate her weight. If she continues to lose weight and becomes really thin then you obviously have to act.

It is not easy to ascertain whether or not an 11 year old is mirroring the body fixation that is part of general society—or if she really is on her way to developing anorexia. If she is developing anorexia it will have a significant impact if the whole family can get together—also the other siblings—and tell her that they understand what is happening. When she understands that everyone is concerned about what is happening and say this to her then her situation is *normalized*. It is very difficult for young people when their parents speak out against body fixation. Children will find it untrustworthy because their parents represent the adult world which is indeed obsessed with the body. They might have heard their mother complain about carrying a few extra kilos or that she has not been able to get the exercise she thinks she needs. She feels fat even though this is far from the truth. Children might hear their mother talk to her friends about the kilos she has put on during the holiday season. When daughters hear this then mothers cannot convincingly tell them that they shouldn't worry about their weight—the worry came from the mothers in the first place.

—*How will they feel about that?*

—Puberty can be a relatively chaotic period of time. Young people often live two different lives:

1. One life which is very emotional and existential.
2. Another life which is social.

Many young people find it both hurtful and offensive when adults only see their social lives and focus solely on the superficial aspects. Then parents are not trustworthy because the fact is that these young people operate on both levels. Besides, there is a constant presence of adults in young people's lives. It is not possible for them to have secrets—neither do they want to. They are living their lives right in front of us—in our faces, as it were. No matter what you think your relationship is like, it is crucial that you try to stay in contact and keep the relationship open.

Stay in contact and keep the relationship open.

—*The so-called "Barbie-injection" contains Melanotan, and is sold illegally. It is meant to tan, decrease your appetite and increase your libido. Boys and girls as young as 13 years old buy it and use it. The side-effects are serious.*

I do my fitness training at a place which has just opened up for 16 year olds. There are girls who cycle for an hour, do pilates for an hour and lift weights for an hour. Three hours of fitness straight after each other. Who has taught our young that it is good to exercise that much?

—Children copy and cooperate. Their focus on exercise will only change years after we adults change our behavior. Children copy the trends of our lives some 10-15 years later. Our obsessive focus on the body went out of control around the turn of the century so it will take time before things change.

It is a huge problem that children today really do not have positive and constructive role models. Politicians everywhere lie, we know that. Every kind of person from priests to police have been found guilty of sexual abuse. Teenage idols are constantly detoxing in drug or alcohol clinics. Mothers talk about their excessive kilos. Obviously, children don't believe adults when they say that looks don't matter. The best—and the only—thing adults can do is to change their lifestyles. When thousands of TV channels spread across the US everyone was able to lean back and have fast food delivered on their doorstep. There are American girls who weigh as much as 180 kgs. The same is happening to their sisters and brothers around the world. As adults we need to start looking inside ourselves: "How trustworthy am I when I speak out against cultural trends? How often do the children hear me worry about my weight? How much money and effort do I dedicate to my personal fitness and well-being?" It is a really good idea to sit down with your children and talk about this. Acknowledge the problem and be prepared to do something about it: "We realize that you believe you are overweight. We acknowledge that we have been part of creating that illusion—we have even contributed to it. We have been living by some of those norms which are really unhealthy. We have some ideas about what can be done so that our family introduces a different lifestyle." Once again, adults have to take responsibility. Parents should not try to play saviors or think they can teach children anything that they do not genuinely believe in themselves. This only exasperates the problem.

> *Obviously, children don't believe adults when they say that looks don't matter. The best—and the only—thing adults can do is to change their lifestyles.*

—How can the family get involved if their daughter develops anorexia, bulimia or becomes a fitness freak. What role does the family play in relation to these illnesses?

—Children and young people who develop symptoms such as anorexia and the like are in an existential crisis. This means that you must do everything you can to avoid focusing on the symptoms. Many parents believe that the problems can been solved if only their daughter begins to eat. This is not so. These children and young people need what I have addressed early in this book—now they just need a lot more of it: They must be taken seriously, acknowledged and seen, and they need to be part of a dialog. If parents have not been able to rid themselves of their own personal self-centeredness then things will get even worse. The family as a unit has a great therapeutic and healing potential. This doesn't mean that you should not seek professional help. I think you should—but many people waste time and money on therapy which doesn't make much difference. If you don't see a great deal of change within a few moths then it is time to go somewhere else. It is important to remember that the family plays an crucial part—alongside professional help. It is not simply the child or the young person who has an problem, it is in fact, the whole family.

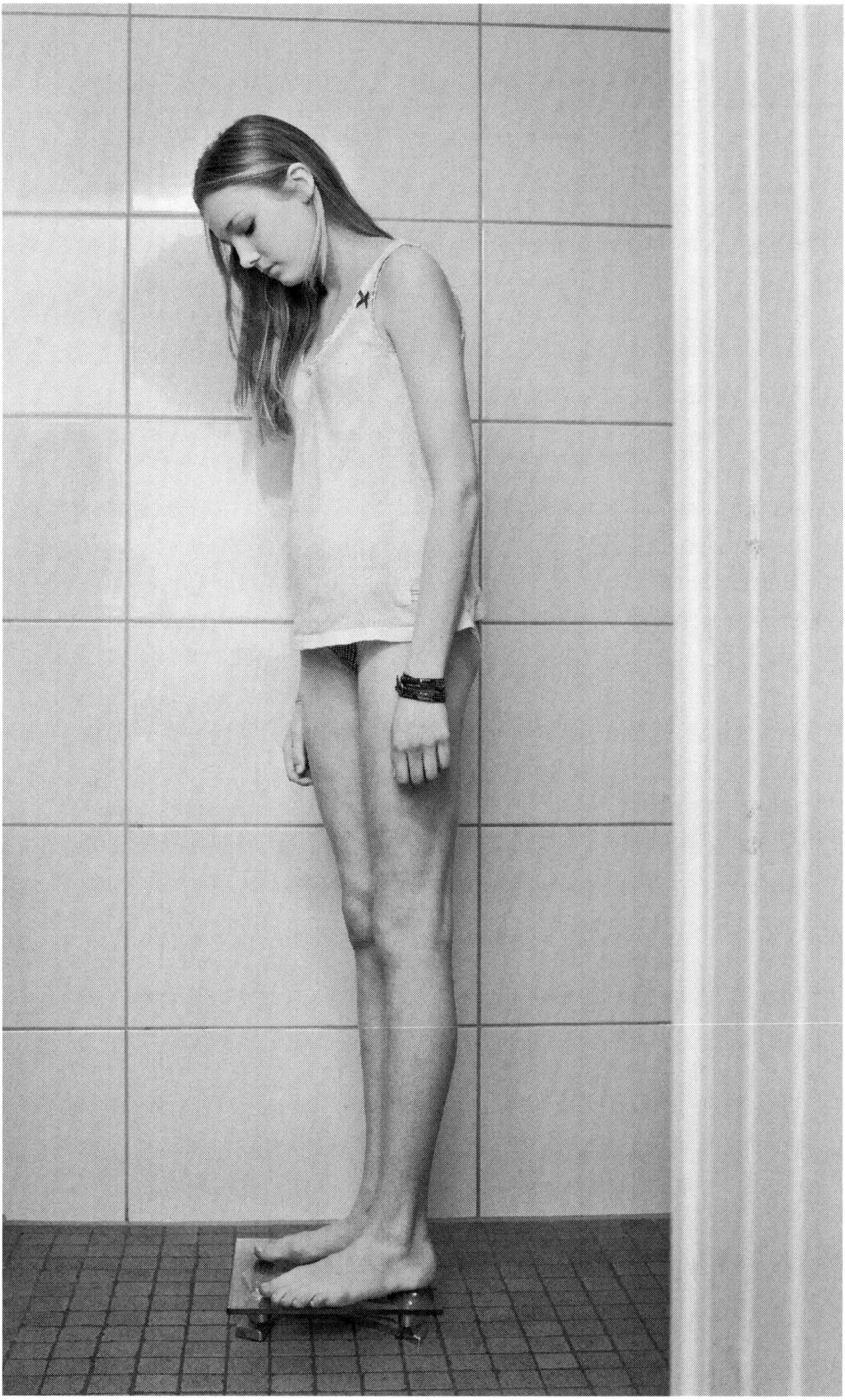

—Is it a collective responsibility?

—Sure. It doesn't do much good simply sending the child or young person to see a psychologist. In one way or another the whole family must be part of the process. In a loving relationship, the whole family will have to relate to the problem. This should be considered a collective responsibility towards each other. However, parents must be mindful not to overdo it. All families experience crises and it is a good idea to be prepared. This is when dialog plays an important part.

A 15 year old girl I met said something very profound. Her parents thought she was bulimic. They were both medical doctors and her father brought home several pamphlets about eating disorders. She didn't want to read them because he had brought them home. The family came to see me and for quite some time the parents spoke about bulimia. Then I asked the daughter: "Are you bulimic or are you not?" She very clearly said: "I am not bulimic!" Then I looked at her parents and said: "Fine, that's that then! She is done!" But they didn't think so. The mother said to her daughter: "I know you trust Jesper. If you prefer to speak with him on your own, then we are happy to pay for that." I quickly interrupted and said that as her mother this was not an appropriate suggestion. She didn't show care for her daughter by offering her psychological help at this point in time. "You have to offer her what you are able to offer as a human being." Then I asked the daughter if she would like to tell her parents what she really needed. She was quiet, searched deep inside and finally said: "A bit more trust would be good." That was the answer.

Everybody wants happy children. There is however, a huge difference between wanting that and turning it into a project. When children become projects they will suffer. Don't ever turn the children into projects!

Family Time

—Perhaps the mother's timing was wrong. Nevertheless, when such a problem arises it is appropriate to speak with the child about psychological help, isn't it? Or do you believe parents want to pass on their responsibility and care?

—If the child says: "What you believe is a problem for me, isn't actually a problem!" then you have to listen and trust. If, in three months time, you still experience the situation as problematic then you might consider doing something.

Imagine if you as an adult would like to strengthen your sense of self-confidence. Every day your husband looks at you with a concerned expression on his face. He tells you that he has read a book about building self-esteem and suggest that you read it. After a couple of months you give up and ask: "Is that all I am: a problem? Or am I more than that?" If you are not able to help yourself in relation to your child you need to tell him or her to let you know if they need help. You should show initiative but it is highly stressful for children if they become the problem.

As parents we worry about our children. This is human nature. Just don't bother the children with your worries. Speak with other adults. Everybody wants happy children. There is however, a huge difference between wanting that and turning it into a project. When children become projects they will suffer. Don't ever turn the children into projects!

A couple of years ago I saw an episode of "Extreme Make-Over" on TV. People went on the show and their looks were completely altered. The lady in the show had no chin, a big nose, browned teeth, thin lips, wrinkles and a number of other things "wrong" with her. These were all cosmetically changed. After the changes, champagne flowed and there was a long applause when the "before and after pictures" were shown.

I too thought it was amazing—until her 12 year old daughter entered to congratulate her mother. She looked exactly like her mother before the changes were made. This is an example of horrible and grotesque role modeling and the media's misuse of the beauty industry. It is also an example of our double standards: we want to be slender and beautiful - and at the same time good role models.

—It is important that our children have the opportunity to mature safely and can feel proud of the way they are—without the media destroying this. How can we allow our children to feel comfortable about intimacy and their own bodies when the world is so superficial and has a body fixation?

—It does help if the parents feel free and comfortable with their own bodies. You need to be—or become—aware of your own boundaries. Are there times when you would rather prefer to be alone? It is alright to say that you prefer to be alone in the bath for example. Children learn how to define their own boundaries when they see how adults do it. When an 11 year old becomes self-conscious and shy about her body you have to respect this. There is no reason to worry about her turning into a spinster or become uncomfortable about her sexuality. I believe this is really important. When they hit puberty the previous 10-12 years of communication will determine if she feels comfortable about asking her mother personal questions. These days our culture is very body fixated and there is a limit to how well we can shield our children from that. We can do a great deal to strengthen their feelings of self and then be available during their difficult times.

—When a teenager reaches the legal age of sexual consent it is difficult for parents to envisage that they might have sexual intercourse. This might even happen in their own home. How much should you expect or hope for them to tell you? To what extent should parents get involved?

—If it is possible to talk about it then this is because you are able to communicate well in many aspects of your lives. I need to emphasize that teenagers will also be fed information from their peers and from the media. Today's eight year old children will know things previous generations didn't find out until they were 40.

Many parents are unsure about how to deal with pornography. I don't have a clear answer to that but I have the feeling that children deal with it quite sensibly. Parents need to remember that their children know a lot about sex but that they are emotionally completely inexperienced. Just like the rest of us they will have to experiment to find some of the answers. Most adults would agree that sex is best when combined with love but how does that make sense to a 15 year old?

Before children reach puberty is it very important that their parents ensure they are able to say: "No!" with a clear conscience. They also need to be able to look after their personal integrity and boundaries. In addition to that it is important that they are able to develop a healthy feeling of self. This enables them to know themselves well enough to say: "Yes!" and "No!" when that is what they really mean.

Parents are most nervous about sexuality that develops during puberty. Even though their sexuality is present and might be practiced much earlier. It is with sexuality as it is with most other aspects of their lives, they need to explore and experiment. This could mean that a 16 year old tries out different things.

> *Show the child the same level of respect as you would an adult.*

If we interviewed one hundred 30 year olds I am convinced that good and healthy sexual relationships are based on positive as well as negative experiences no matter what age they started. If your 11 year old looks at pornography on the Internet you need to be diplomatic. There is a significant difference between *being seen* and *being found out*. It is important that parents understand this difference. It is also important to say: "Listen, I have noticed (this and that) and I have some opinions about that. Would you like to hear what I would like to say?" If he says: "No!" you just say: "Okay, then I will wait and try again another day. Let me know if you want to know what I would like to say." In case he says: "No!" two more times you need to cut to the chase and say: "I am very anxious to tell you what is on my mind, so now I have to tell you." It is all about showing the child the same level of respect as you would an adult.

—If you happen to see your child masturbate is it better to ignore it and pretend you didn't see it?

—Yes, I think so. It is important that they are allowed to do it. Even small children explore their sexuality and parents need not worry or fear that it is abnormal. Hopefully, the child care center will support this. Of course they need to make sure it doesn't happen while others are present. "You just need to leave the others and be alone if you need to do it." Many adults are unsure about children and sexuality simply because hardly anyone can remember masturbating as three or five year olds. We remember puberty.

A number of good books are available. They give an overview over what is normal at different stages of their development. Some adults can remember episodes from their own childhoods when they were blamed, made to feel guilty or even punished for exploring their sexuality. In my opinion it is important to consider the individual's sexuality, sensuality and eroticism as something pleasurable instead of something problematic.

Speaking about sexuality might not be easy during puberty. These conversations need to happen throughout their childhood and youth.

—To be a good parent do you have to be the one talking to your children about sexuality?

—You cannot assume that the children want to speak with you or their teachers about sexuality. In Denmark, groups of young people around the age of 25 were trained and travelled around to schools and spoke about sexuality. That worked because children felt comfortable about asking those young adults. Years ago schools were charged with the duty to inform students about sexuality and "the birds and the bees". In theory this is fine but many students have clearly expressed that they find it uncomfortable talking about such intimate issues with someone who later will be teaching them Maths—or who might give them a detention. How big a part parents can play depends on their relationship. It is my impression that most of their knowledge primarily comes from friends, books, magazines and the Internet.

—Instead of loading children with information parents should rather invite them to ask if there is something they would like to know more about?

—Sure, you could do that. It is good for them to know that they can ask either of their parents about these things. I believe it is a really good idea to speak about the differences between the sexuality which they can experience a result of a loving relationship and the mechanisms of the sexuality that they can experience through pornography. Some really good books are available and they can be made accessible at home. I am saddened that our culture no longer has initiation celebrations which mark milestones such as the first menstruation.

—*A mother once told me how difficult it was for her to talk with her daughter about menstruation. The mother calculated that her daughter might menstruate during a school camp and suggested that she carried some pads. The daughter didn't think this was necessary. "Okay," said the mother "I'll just put some in the bathroom." The daughter took the pads and they came in handy. I thought it was a great way of dealing with the issue.*

—I agree. The mother respected her daughter's integrity.

—*It can be challenging for young people to define their boundaries and say: "No!" to adult's "invasions". How can they learn this if they are not taught at home? At a number of schools in Scandinavia the children in 2nd grade massage each other in order for them to be able to say: "Stop!" if it starts hurting.*

—There are many good things about cultures where adults don't just push in but instead ask if they can have a kiss or a hug.

—*I recall a little boy who didn't react very positively when an adult played rough and tumble with him.*

Family Time

—Children react completely differently to physical contact. Some love cuddles, being close to others and sitting on your lap. It is just fine. My grandson Alex is not like that at all. Not every eight to ten year old child feels comfortable about closeness.

—*There is nothing wrong with children if they don't want to sit on your lap?*

—No, not at all! They have to find out how close is too close. Some adults don't like physical closeness, and we all respect that. Children learn to relate appropriately to their own sexuality when it is a natural part of their upbringing—and when they learn to define their personal boundaries.

Parents can tell their children that sex is beautiful and important, that there is no reason to feel ashamed about their sexuality and emotions, and that it is a good idea to talk about these things with someone important. Parents also need to tell them that sex is not something we share with everybody. Parents need to learn about each individual child and ensure that the physical closeness it not experienced as a violation.

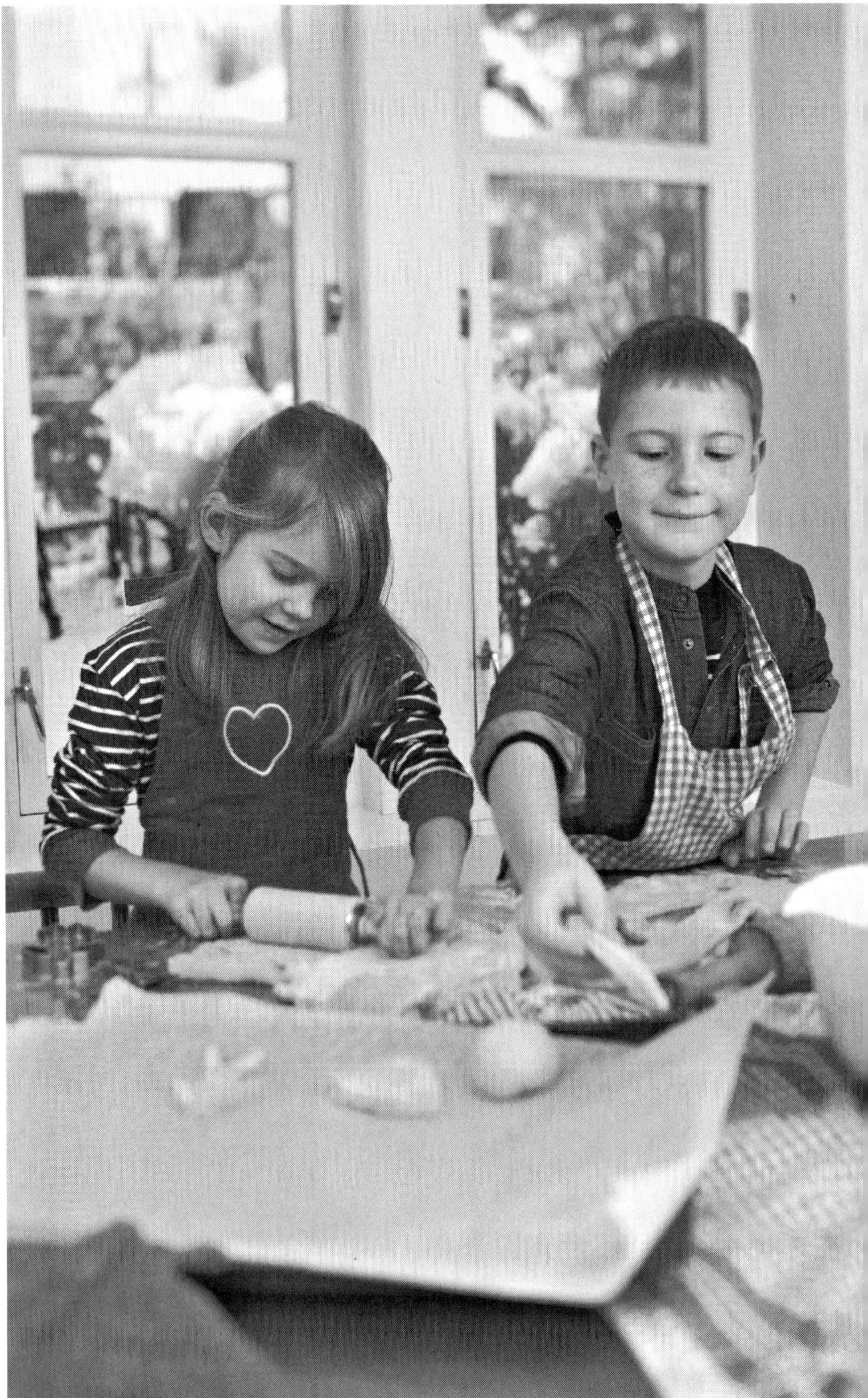

THE KITCHEN
– Food and conversation

The kitchen is often the room where the different family members first get together in the morning. This is where tea or coffee is brewed, lunches are prepared, dinner is cooked, plates are cleaned and many other tasks are completed. It is also the room where family members meet to talk and where visitors are welcomed. At the end of the day it is a good place for a snack and to let the day settle before bedtime.

MONICA:
—The kitchen might be one of the most important areas of the house. I am thinking of the kitchen's importance for atmosphere. What is it like when you get up and leave in the morning? A good start to the day, what does that mean?

JESPER:
—It is first and foremost a start without too much stress. It is easy to run into conflicts though. Children need to dress, have breakfast, brush teeth, prepare lunch, pack bags, and this is often a time when

parents' struggle to show leadership. Most of the conflicts occur because the parents are too busy. There is a significant difference between the adult's pace and that of the children – especially those under five years old. Things often go severely wrong when adults insist that children keep pace with them. Children's natural response to this is to slow down even further. The more stressed adults are—the slower children become. Many children have expressed that they feel like *little parcels*. They are lifted out of bed, carried into the bathroom, dressed, taken to the breakfast table and so forth. They don't like being treated this way—so they protest. However, it is okay to tell your child that it is necessary to hurry. You might say: *"I know you don't like it when we have to rush but you will be able to live with that."* It is fine to use you own adult language when speaking with a one or two year old. They might not understand everything but they get the main message, namely: *"My parents have taken responsibility for this and they need me to adjust."* Then children will do as best they can—but not every day!

—*Perhaps the mother is very busy in the morning so she gets angry over the smallest things. Let's say the daughter forgets her lunchbox on the kitchen bench. In the car the mother gets really angry and yells at her daughter. Later she regrets this. Has any harm been done?*

—The situation you describe is perfectly fine. No harm has been done to anyone.

—*Wouldn't it be better if the mother explains why she gets angry?*

—You might need to be irrational 50 times before you are able to be rational and explain the situation. It is worse if the mother says to her daughter: "Last night I told you that I had to get to work early. You never listen and it is impossible to explain things to you. You just spoil things all the time." All the mother says (and all the child hears) is: "you-you-you-you . . ." Things will go wrong. In your example the mother got angry and yelled which might frighten her daughter. She will in turn learn something about her mother.

The situation is similar in relation to your partner. If you are in a hurry and you partner isn't ready you could say: "Right, we spoke about leaving together but I am too stressed. Let's go separately!" You present him with a solution to the dilemma instead of creating a new one – which would happen if you said: "We had agreed to leave together but now you are making things difficult..!"

As humans we are geared to consider and value our community. We worry that our marriage is a failure if we eat separately, sleep in different rooms because it gives us a better rest, and so forth. We need to look at this differently. Finding solutions which work for the family is positive—even if these solutions don't follow the norms and traditions we think are the right ones.

—I was taught not to read at the table. In spite of this, it sometimes happens in our family because we want peace and quiet or because we want to wake up slowly.

—My wife and I often write in the mornings. I might write three columns between 6 am and 7:30 am. We are at our different laptops and actually find this quite intimate. My mother always said that we had to have breakfast together in our family. For my wife and I this would have been a useless compromise because none of us would get what we really needed.

—Imagine mother and daughter in the kitchen. The daughter is being shown how to cook pancakes. There is a great atmosphere and the daughter is ready to start. The mother says: "No, not like

that. You need to do it like this! You need more butter..!" The tension rises, the daughter storms out and everything is ruined. How do you solve a situation like that?

—The purpose of exploring as part of any learning process means that things have to go wrong. This is exactly what enables us to learn. In your example the mother could have said: "I notice that you do it like that, would you like some help?" Then the child will most likely ask: "Am I doing it the wrong way?" to which the mother answers: "I am not sure if it is wrong but you do it differently to the way I would have done it." Perhaps she tells you that she wants to do it her way. Then you can say: "Alright, but if I am going to eat any of the pancakes then . . ." It is important for parents to be both honest and loving. It is just fine to tell her that you do not like the pancakes when they are made in a certain way or that you prefer them cooked with more butter, less sugar, or whatever. You will not be criticizing your daughter. You tell her that you like them better in a different way—not that she hasn't done things the right way.

It is about social competence. Unfortunately, we often get this completely wrong because we are taught that it is *selfish* to say: "I". This is in fact, the most *selfless* word you can say. When you tell your daughter that you prefer pancakes with more butter then she knows where you stand. This creates confidence and a sense of security, and can only happen through honest and loving responses. People need to be able to both hear and say this. It is also useful in the workforce. You might be able to say to your boss: "When you become stressed like that I worry that it is because of me." The boss cannot guess that this is how you feel, so you have to say it.

You can only feel a sense of security when you are given an honest and loving response. People need to be able to both hear and say this.

Most of us do get stressed at work and at home. During the day we are parents, colleagues and friends for nine or more hours. After work, family life begins again. We quickly become frustrated—especially if we realize that we cannot cope. I think it is wonderful to prepare delicious meals but sometimes a cheese sandwich will have to suffice. I want to talk to my family, tell them about my day, listen to theirs and vent what is on my mind.

—What should our priorities be in regards to the family meals?

—If you expect that your family will always get on well during meal times then you will be disappointed. Discussions and silly arguments will happen simply because we are all different. Things will also go wrong if everyone is in a hurry, guzzles the food down in different places around the house. This will hurt the younger children in particular because food plays such a central and symbolic role in their lives. Food is love. Women experience this while they breast-feed or bottle-feed. For children food is care. Food is really our strongest symbol of love. Love is our first need and it is fulfilled through food and closeness. As adults we also experience this if we invite a date over for dinner. It is a vote of confidence.

> *Food is love. Women experience this while they breast-feed or bottle-feed. For children food is care. Food is really our strongest symbol of love.*

It is not right to say that family meal times don't matter much—because they matter to children. It is important to put an effort in. If you have to answer the phone during dinner then you ought to excuse yourself and tell the family that this is a one-off. If, on the other hand, it is a one-off that the family has dinner together then you will pay a price later on. The dinner table is often a good place to bring up issues that need to be spoken about. The less time you have to bring up conflicts the more conflicts will occur as there are not many other opportunities for family gatherings. If you don't eat together very often you will easily be met with a whole series of conflict when you finally do. This is a clear signal that it is a good idea to spend more time together.

—*You are saying that if the family prioritizes social settings such as dinners then everyone will be better at handling conflicts?*

—Absolutely! We need to be cautious if we are thinking that a good meal is one where everyone feels good and everything is harmonious. During meal times parents have the opportunity to find out how their children are. If you impose a certain atmosphere you will never gain access to this valuable information. Then you will inevitably be surprised when the school rings up and tells you about a problem.

—*Would it be a good idea to ask everyone around the table if there is something they would like to talk about?*

—Sure, that would be fine but it is important that the adults begin. Children don't thrive so well when they are the center of attention. Things go terribly wrong when parents sit and stare at the children while they are having dinner. You can try this out with a young child who continually throws things on the floor. If you say: "No! Stop doing that!" and then turn around continuing what you were doing. The child will most likely stop doing it. If you instead stare at the child it will continue doing it.

You might remember what it was like meeting your in-laws-to-be for the first time. It was highly uncomfortable knowing that you were under observation. When you are the center of attention you cannot be part of the community.

Family Time

—There are children who continue throwing things and think it is exciting even though their parents don't look at them. Is the throwing of food very common among small children?

—When they are between one and two it is very common simply because it is a game and it is fun. Children at that age have no idea that food is not for playing with. You will see this when they drop or throw a spoon. The parents will pick it up. Throwing food is just another game for them. They only realize that there is a difference when they turn three or four years old. Then they realize that they shouldn't do that. If you would like to stop it you could say: "I don't want to play that game any longer." Perhaps your child will continue but all you need is a bit of patience.

—How do you teach children proper table manners, such as using a knife and fork?

—Children love to copy their parents. Most small children want to use a knife and fork before they are able to handle them properly. It takes time to learn and the more you correct them the longer it takes. Research has clearly showed this. According to a recent research study it will take twice the amount of time for a child to learn proper table manners when they are taught how to instead of simply being able to copy their parents. When parents eat properly their children will also do so. In regards to table manners you might need to say to the child that it is better to eat at the table than on the floor. It doesn't make any sense to the child if they are told that it is wrong to sit on the floor.

—Are you saying that there is no point in commenting if a child licks their fingers or eats the food with their fingers.

—It is alright to comment on these things but there are different ways of saying it. You could just say what you would like: "I would like you to use your fork and not just your fingers." or "Can you do me a favor and use both hands when you lift your glass?" These are example of good communication. It is not a good idea to tell the child to do this, that or the other, or "it is bad manners if you . . ." or something like that.

My grandson is a typical example. He is just like his father—my son. Many of the challenges I met when my son was young, I see in my grandson. He has insisted on feeding himself since he was seven months old. He also wants to eat exactly the same things as we adults do. He really enjoys Croatian national dishes with both chili and garlic. When he was younger he would take some very big bites. Then he would try to chew them, take them out of his mouth and place them next to his plate. My son did exactly the same when he was young and it really frustrated me. He and I fought about this for years without me ever thinking of just placing a smaller plate next his dinner plate. In relation to my grandson I was personal and clear: "Alex, I don't want you to put your food on the table if you don't want to eat it. You will have to put it back on the plate." He looked at me for a while and picked it up. He put it on his plate and looked at me again as if he needed to find out if that was what I meant. I said: "Yes, that's what I mean. Thank you!" We did this three times in one week before he turned 12 months and since then he hasn't put his half-eaten food on the table.

The more critical the teaching environment the less anyone is able to learn. This applies to learning of social activities as well as academic learning. Raising children while there is food on the table ruins the meal for everyone—including the parents. Many men are criticized by their wives and lose the interest in food as well as the community. It is worth considering how much energy the adults waste because they are not personal and don't clearly say what they want. When I was young my parents said: "That's not the way you do it. Do this . . . !"

Family Time

—They gave you orders?

—Exactly! It is not possible for a child to know how to—or not to—do things. Researchers have found that in a learning environment dominated by criticism children will only hear around 20% of what they would in a better environment. Children have always known this—now researchers know it as well. It is essential that both new and experienced teachers learn this too!

Some parents try to hold onto as much power as they can. One is that the children must learn about consequences. In the Norwegian newspaper, *Aftonposten*, I answered a question posed by a grandmother. Her daughter, son-in-law and their three year old grandson came for a visit. The whole family had dinner together and the dad decided that the boy had to stay at the table until everyone had finished. They had entrée and mains—and an hour passes. The boy asked if he could go out and play. "No!" said the father. "You have to stay here otherwise you won't get any dessert." The boy slowly slid off his chair and went out to play. Half an hour later he returned. He had forgotten all about his father's rule and saw a delicious cake on the table. He asked for a piece but his father said: "No!" The grandmother wrote to me how she experience this: "I had just taken my fist bite when the boy asked. It was as if that little bite in my mouth grew bigger and bigger. I considered how I could sabotage my own daughter and her husband's upbringing and hide a piece of cake in the fridge and give it to the boy later."

I wrote to the grandmother and told her that this situation was based on a misunderstanding—one which happens all the time. The couple would like their son to understand that his actions have *consequences*. Had the boy stayed at the table and asked for his third or fourth piece of cake they could have said to him: "Listen, if you eat four pieces of cake you will get a pain in your stomach!" Had he chosen to eat his fourth piece and had his stomach started to ache that would have been a *consequence*. Denying him cake unless he stays at the table and calling that a *consequence* is a mistake and has nothing to do with *consequence*. That is called *punishment*.

—*So . . . it is not a good idea to use "consequences" as part of raising the boy when he is able to experience things for himself and learn from that straight away?*

—What the father does in this example is punish the boy. This has nothing to do with *consequences*. He calls it a *consequence* in order to justify his actions. There is no consequence in real life—outside that family's environment—that says: "if you leave the table you cannot have dessert". That is not reality. I believe it is important to think carefully about the difference between *consequences* and *punishment*. Most parents don't think they punish their children. They try to be as responsible as they can. They don't do it to be tough or because they dislike their children—they just try to be good parents.

—*Perhaps many do it in good faith? We think of children as being inexperienced and that it is our duty to teach them about life. Does it happen also because we as parents complicate things and stress too much?*

—Many parents think it is difficult having children. While the children are young most parent struggle more than is necessary. When a couple have their first child they go on a crash course in leadership, self-confidence and feelings of self. It is perfectly alright not being able to master everything from the start, but it is possible to learn this within a few years—as long as they don't think they are lacking certain methods or techniques. What they are lacking is a

Family Time

voice that makes an impression—one that children feel comfortable with. Contrary to what many "experts" will tell you, children don't need *upbringing*. What they need is guidance with empathy. It is a good idea to consider children as if they come from another planet. They don't understand this world and need some guidance.

> *Contrary to what many "experts" will tell you, children don't need upbringing. What they need is guidance with empathy.*

—*Who should set the table and tidy up afterwards? Who should prepare the lunches?*

—If nobody likes to prepare meals on their own—or no one has the time to do it—then everyone has to help out. If you don't want to do it on a particular day then it is your responsibility to find someone who can sit in for you. At a very early stage children really want to prepare their own lunches. Let them do it. Children are fully capable of being responsible for their own lunches at the time they start school.

I read a police report about youth and alcohol. This was presented to my son's school. I am sure it applies to most schools anywhere in the world. It was full of frightening observations and statistics about children's substance abuse, drugs and alcohol. One of the questions many parents struggle with is whether or not to let their children have alcohol at home. The research shows that those children who try alcohol with their parents' permission drink more and are worst off. The police report I saw showed many cases of excessive use, overdoses and the need for pumping out. Many parents are at a loss. We always try to do the best for our children.

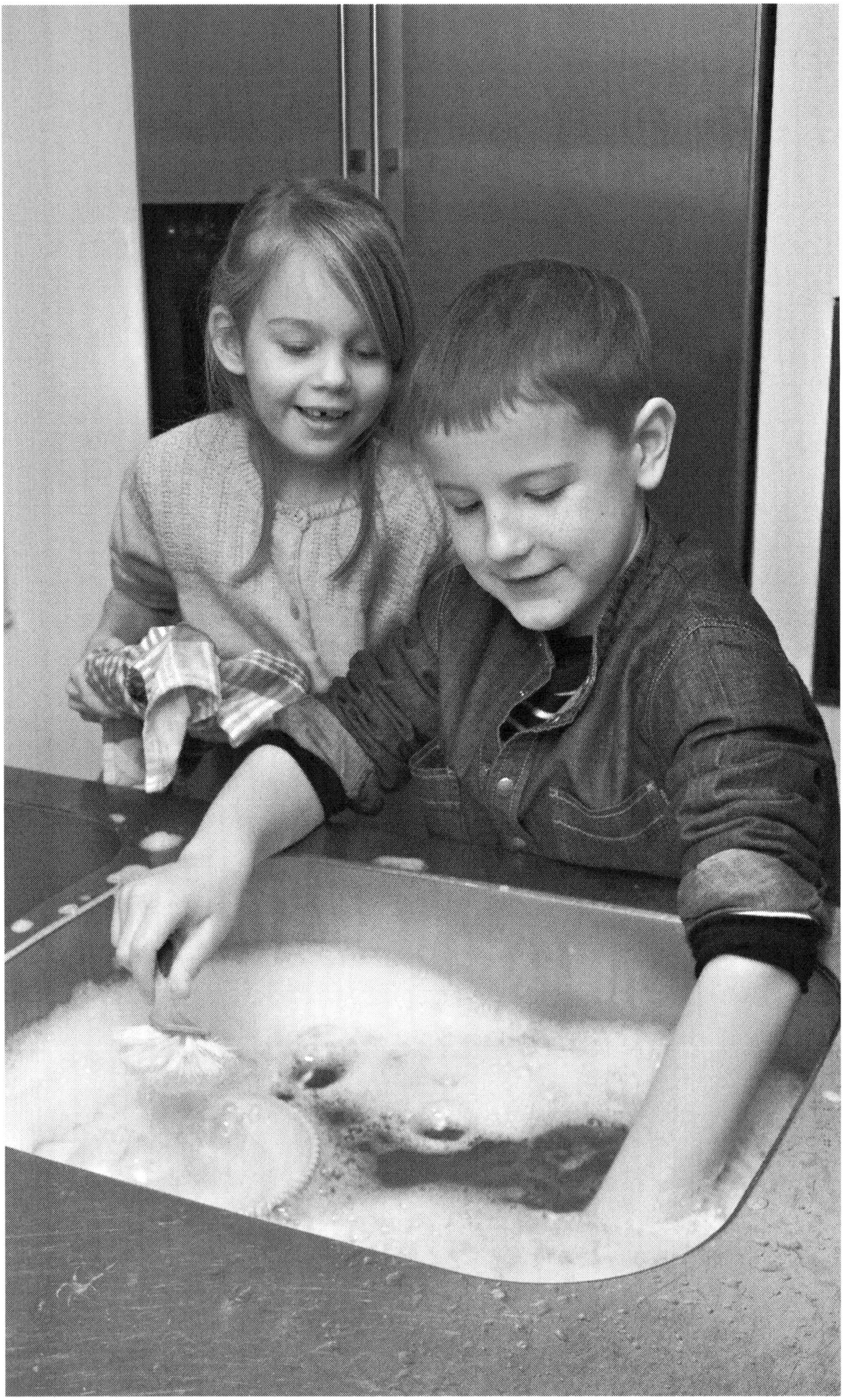

—In Norway we saw a campaign aimed at parents suggesting they should not buy alcohol for their children because it only adds to the alcohol the children already buy themselves. What do you think about that?

—Parents can buy alcohol if this is part of the family's decision regarding alcohol. However, they should not buy alcohol for children to drink on their own. If your son is 17 years old, has invited friends to a party and you have said that it is alright for them to drink, then you have created the expectation that you buy the alcohol. However, you must obviously abide by the law. In a number of countries it is illegal to buy and serve alcohol to children under a certain age.

There is a serious difference between drinking alcohol at 14 and at 17 years of age. Research shows that alcohol does more harm to the brain the younger the children are.

The statistics showing that children who try alcohol with their parents' permission are worst off might have to do with a number of issues. Part of this also has to do with social status, the amount of money available to young people, the amount of alcohol consumed by their parents' and other adults, and so forth. It is very unusual to be invited out for dinner without also being served alcohol.

—Do you think that things which are forbidden or we have limited access to attract a certain curiosity? Is that one of the reasons why children become interested and eager to try it out?

—Absolutely! Everything that is forbidden will always be interesting. Thereby it has the complete opposite effect of what their parents had hoped for.

—Do you think it is okay for parents to enjoy alcohol at dinner time while the children are there? Some people feel strongly about this?

—Children will not be harmed by watching their parents enjoy a glass—as long as "a glass" doesn't mean one glass too many. If your alcohol consumption alters your reactions and behaviors (e.g., .05 blood alcohol concentration) then children will be impacted upon—they won't know where you stand. When parents use alcohol in an effort to ease their stress levels, anxiety or conflicts they will definitely provide a basis for the children's own abuse. Exactly the same happens when conflicts are resolved by the use of violence. Children simply copy our adult behavior—or dissociate themselves completely. Adults don't need to stop drinking out of consideration for the children but we should avoid getting drunk—at least until they are almost adults. It is never good for children or young people to see their parents drunk but when they are almost adults it will no longer harm them.

—What do you think about sweet things? Sugar is also a stimulant and it is highly addictive. When I grew up we were given a bag of sweets only on Saturdays otherwise we would harm our teeth. How restrictive should today's parents be with sweet things and soft drinks?

—My son and his wife also asked me about sugar when their son, Alex was born. I could only say this: "Keep sugar away from him for the first three years." Sugar is harmful to small children. It increases the blood sugar level to the point of hyperactivity—then it drops below normal levels. When they get close to the level of depression they need more to get back on top. The consumption of sugar and soft drings is on a steady increase and today some children drink more than one and a half liters of soft drink every day. That is abuse! It makes the brain function in a strange and abnormal manner. Most children are able to monitor and control their level of sugar intake if they are taught how.

I wish food manufacturers would stop adding sugar to the products they claim are healthy. Look at your breakfast serials for example. This is a serious health issue and politicians neglected their moral responsibility when they passed the problem to parents so they could deal with it instead of making the manufacturers accountable.

—Sometimes I feel that I have been too dogmatic instead of considering the circumstances and the situation.

—That is one way of doing it. I believe that aiming to be *consistent* is an absurd goal. This means you are not being influenced by others. The logical conclusion of this means that you will not change your opinion and you will be thinking the same in five years as you are today. There is no reason to be consistent just for the sake of it. Neither should children have chores just for the sake of doing chores. It has to make sense for it to be realistic.

—I grew up with the idea that consistency is important even if it didn't always make sense. Rules need to be adhered to—not to be broken.

—We need to ask ourselves what kind of children we would like. Do we want children who are able to live in the real world? Some believe that an organized and disciplined life is the only way to bring up safe and confident children. That is absolutely and completely wrong. In the late 1990s I held a seminar for a group of schoolteachers who insisted that their students had to eat the crusts of their sandwiches at lunchtime. I just did not understand why. Children do not develop self-esteem or self-confidence through discipline. It concerns me greatly when so many people believe that children feel safe and confident when they have to follow those kinds of rules. They force children who do not like crusts to eat them.

—They might think that crusts are full of nutrition or good for the teeth?

—Obviously, people try to justify their behavior. I think Norway is the only place in the world where the issue of eating the crust has become a national ideology and matter of principle. Of course, the crusts aren't the problem but the fact this myth has become a "truth" by popular hype—other cultures have their own idiosyncrasies.

Let us focus a little bit more on the idea of being *consistent* with children. The reason for the focus on this ideology is based on research conducted between the 1930s and 1980s. Researchers found that children who developed problems more often than not came from homes with *in*consistent parents. The problem however, was not that the parents changed their minds. The problem was that they lacked values. They did not have a set of values upon which to base their decision-making. When you as an adult feel confident with the values you have then you will intuitively know what to reject and what to accept. You will no longer feel the need to be *consistent* in your decisions but *consistent* in basing them on one set of values. Many parents already feel confident following their values but those who constantly feel the need to consider what the next-door neighbor might think are not *consistent*. Children will notice this difference while the experts only see it as *inconsistency*.

Let your children make their own decisions. If your son says: "No!" to one of his friends you could wait for an hour and ask him: "You said: "No!" to your friend before, was that a good decision?" Let him have options and allow him to change his mind.

It is a paradox that parents often criticize their children for being *consistent* even though this is exactly what they do themselves. Your son might go next door to play with his friend. If the neighbor's boy doesn't want to play his parents will probably invite your son inside anyway—one must be well-mannered when visitors arrive. Following this, their son becomes stubborn and does not want to do anything at all. His parents will criticize him for not changing his mind because he is *consistent* in his rejection.

—*How can we help our children make good choices? Some are insecure, vague and need guidance, while others have a strong determination and know what they want. How can we help them?*

—Let your children make their own decisions. If your son says: "No!" to one of his friends you could wait for an hour and ask him: "You said "No!" to your friend before, was that a good decision?" Let him have options and allow him to change his mind. When children have to defend their decisions some will become even more insecure. We shouldn't criticize children who speak their minds.

I know many people who use bribes to make their children stop eating sugary things. If they do not have any sugary things for a certain period of time they are rewarded. This is an interesting idea but I cannot help thinking that the children live in the real world—and part of that world is sugar and sweet things.

It is not easy motivating our children to think about health, carbohydrates, blood sugar, GI and so forth. Children spit out the food they don't like. It is very frustrating when we try to make them eat healthy food.

—How can we teach our children to take responsibility for their own diet so they understand that it is their own body and health which suffers when they make unfortunate decisions in regards to food, fat and sugar?

—I have written about this in my book, "Smile! Dinner is ready." It is clear that children's attitude to food and diet first and foremost depends on their parents' attitude to this. Secondly, it depends on the parents' ability to create a good atmosphere around the table. Thirdly, it is important to remember that food and the use of force do not go together.

Even when children eat predominantly healthy food during the first seven years of their lives we cannot avoid that they also eat unhealthy things—especially during puberty.

Our children's attitude to food doesn't really present itself until they start their own families. Then you will know how many and which of your values they hang on to. That is very different from being a teenager and visiting McDonald's—it might not be so cool going to a macrobiotic restaurant. It is during the student years that many eat very poorly.

It is almost impossible to see the difference between a 14 year old girl who is looking after herself and eats healthy food, and one who is developing an eating disorder. We have a new eating disorder amongst young women who are so focused on eating healthy food that they become ill or die of malnutrition. Parents must do as best they can during their children's first 10 to 12 years, after that it is up to the children themselves. For a teenager McDonald's might be an important social setting. I believe this is a sensible priority and in this situation it is more important than nutrition.

—Children have so many choices. They are also influenced by advertising.

—Some people argue that children have too many options. This is true if you are a mother who doesn't know what you would like for dinner so you leave it up to the child. This is completely different from asking the child what he or she would like for dinner.

—What about those parents who read this and feel that they have got everything completely wrong? Is there still hope after the child turns 10 years old?

—Yes, there is plenty of hope—and I cannot repeat this often enough! The best parents I have ever met make around 15 to 20 mistakes every day. Those who make more than 50 mistakes do need support. Children understand that their parents are not capable of everything. What they don't understand is why they have to be punished when their mother or father cannot make a decision. Parents who are not able to assert personal authority, define their boundaries and say: "No!" in relation to their children are not able to do this in their relationships with other adults either. Children don't have the necessary experiences so they think: "What is going on? I really want to make my mother happy but what does she want? Does she want to eat what I feel like?"

During the first 15 years as a family therapist I never met a family who had problems with their children's eating habits. This, and a few other things, such as bedtime, have become serious challenges for the post-modern family. The question is: "How can parents show the leadership that the children need without violating them?" When *insecurity* becomes part of parents' identity then children will not thrive.

In my family I am the one who does the shopping. I shop without asking my wife what she would like. Every now and then I have so many other things on my mind that I will ask her what she would like for dinner. Then I might buy whatever she asked for—or something completely different. I don't let go of the leadership. When parents ask their children what they would like they add a very strange logic—one which they do not use in relation to other adults. This logic tells them that they cannot say: "No!" once they have asked. If parents ask their son what he would like for dinner and for the third day in a row he says he would like pizza then many parents believe that they cannot say: "No!" This is absurd. If I ask you what time it would suit you for us to meet, then I don't *have* to be able to meet you at that time. It ought to be like that when children say they want pizza for dinner. The parents might think it is alright to have pizza again and again or they should ask him to suggest something else. If he doesn't suggest any alternatives then the parents must decide what is for dinner. Sure, their son will be frustrated but he will get over that very soon—unless the parents hang over him trying to convince him that he is wrong and they are right. Then he will become stubborn and say: "Don't tell me it is wrong for me to want pizza because you asked me and that is what I want!"

—Many parents try to be cool and be on the side of their children. Perhaps they fear that their children will challenge them and not like them as parents?

—Once again I must remind you that many parents choose "the road of least resistance". The conversation goes like this:

Mother: "What would you like for dinner?"
Son: "Pizza!"
Father: "No, we eat too much pizza."
Son: "I WANT PIZZA!"

Family Time

Mother: "Alright . . . ! You can have your pizza!"

The parents want peace at any cost. When you look at the upper and upper-middle classes of our society you will find many parents like that. Their children often end up in trouble. It is obviously not good for children to eat a lot of chocolate—no matter how much they like it. It is better for them to become frustrated and get the nutrition they need. Children cannot develop the necessary competencies, vitality and emotions without being frustrated every now and then. Frustrations are part of the learning process. Imagine working somewhere or being in a relationship and hoping for someone to come and save you as soon as you become frustrated! That won't happen.

—Is it possible to solve that dilemma? How do we get children to eat healthy food without all the fuss?

—I have a number of friends who are excellent chefs. They are not so keen on having sausages or fish and chips on their menus. They have asked me what they should do when guests ask for a "kids menu". I tell them not to give in! Instead they become creative and try to accommodate the children in different ways. One of these chefs told me that when children come to his restaurant and don't like what is on the menu he invites them to the kitchen. He shows them the ingredients and asks them to come up with ideas for a new dish. The children immediately change their attitude and become more interested. Their parents wonder what the chef does. The answer is very simple: he takes the children seriously. The same chef was booked to cook for a confirmation party. He sat with the parents to discuss the menu and they would tell him all about the different things their son didn't like. So he asked to speak with the young man himself and asked what he would like. He wanted pizza! The chef said that he didn't make pizza and told him this: "Do you know that if you eat pizza more than five times a months then you will lose more tennis matches?" He used an argument from the boy's world and after an hour of negotiations the menu was set. The chef used his authority as a chef and defined his boundaries. Then the boy cooperated. It can be as simple as that. It can also become difficult especially if you try to be *child-friendly* and fear entering into a genuine dialog with the child. That only results in discussions and negotiations that parents rarely win.

—Once again you stress the importance of NOT treating children and young people any differently from the way we would treat adults.

—You are right, that is what I am saying. Many people strongly disagree with me. In 2005 I was interviewed by a Danish journalist about going on holiday with children. I said: "Forget about going on *child-friendly* holidays!" You should obviously not go on a holiday and pretend the children aren't there but if you love art museums then bring the children along. There is no point in planning a holiday depending on what is enjoyable for two or three year olds. Parents make a big mistake if they think they are self-centered when they do things they like to do. It is exactly these kind of parents who children need as role models. Children have a desperate need for learning what it is like to be an adult. When parents only do *child-friendly* activities, only serve *child-friendly* menus and so forth, the children will never learn. The challenge of being *child-friendly* means to include them in your decisions and plans, it doesn't mean that you let them set the agenda.

> *Parents make a big mistake if they think they are self-centered when they do things they like to do. It is exactly these kind of parents who children need as role models.*

—*There are so many books and different opinions about how to raise children. What we all hope for is to live good lives? A good atmosphere at home and a good flow of communication. Isn't that more important than any theory and principle?*

—*Atmosphere* is probably the most important aspect for children. Look after the *atmosphere!* A parent who is in the kitchen and cooking with joy and enthusiasm creates an excellent atmosphere which attracts children like a magnet. Let them come to you. Give them things to do without turning it into a serious and organized pedagogical project. The good atmosphere will be part of the meal and at the table. Just remember that *good* atmosphere doesn't mean a *harmonious* atmosphere. A good atmosphere in the family reflects the way every member feels at that point in time. Some days things happen which make the atmosphere heavy or high—and that is just fine.

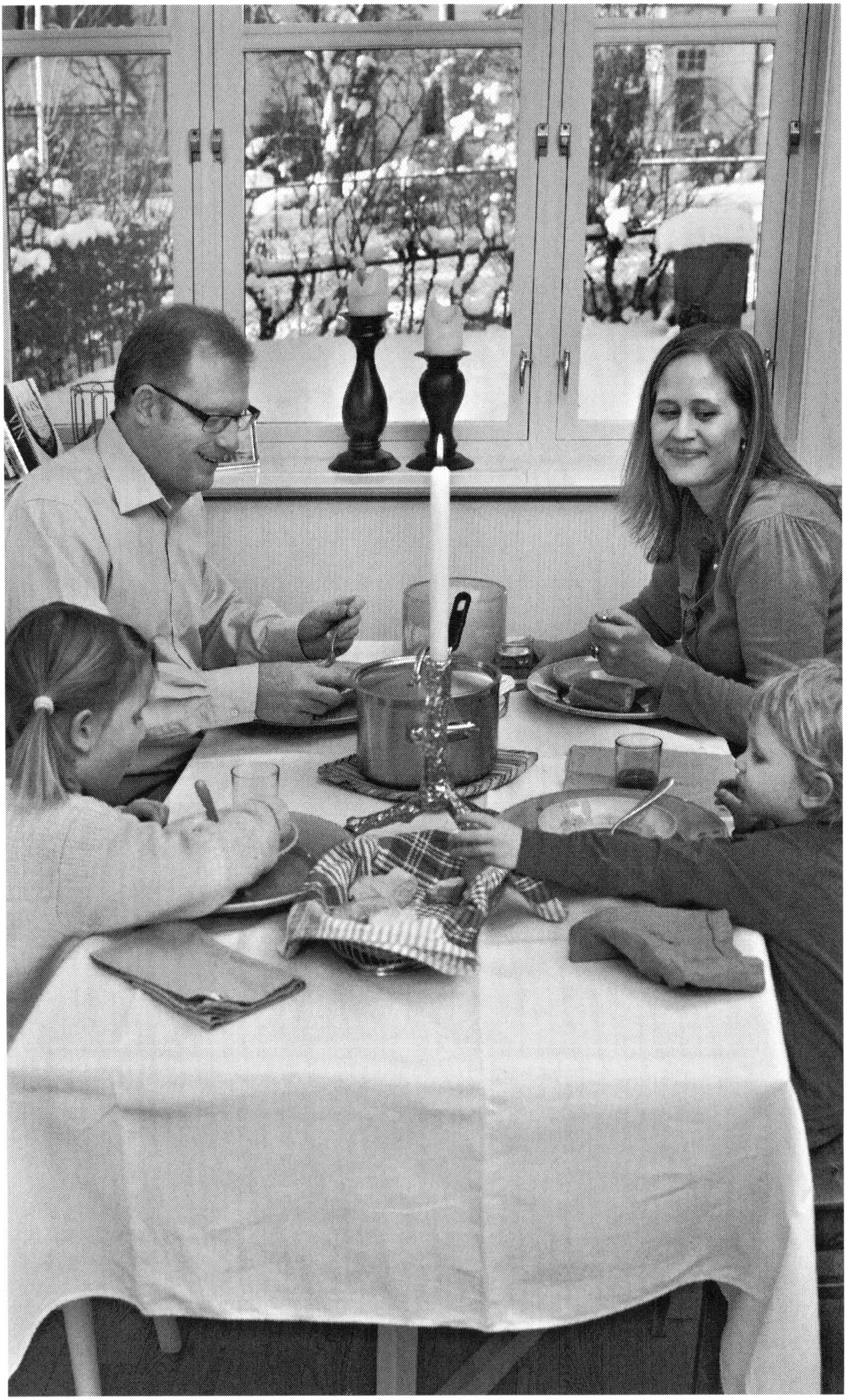

THE LIVING ROOM
– Community and atmosphere

"Atmosphere" is very important for children. But what creates a good atmosphere? What makes a room nice to be in? Does it depend on the colors on the walls, the furniture or the people? I believe we could be in any room, and indeed anywhere in the world, and feel a good atmosphere—as long as we feel valued by those we are with. We must be able to argue, cry, laugh and love . . . we must be able to be ourselves.

MONICA:
—*Communication is challenging. The most recent generation of families has been called "negotiation families". Everything has to be negotiated.*

JESPER:
—This is a consequence of democratization. There is a difference between discussions and dialogs. Essentially, discussions are about winning. Dialogs are different. They are not about winning or losing, neither do they focus on convincing another person about

anything. Instead, they are all about exploring who we are and what we want. Dialog can be described like this: If one person makes a statement then the next person can build on that, and so forth. Instead of agreeing or disagreeing we let ourselves be inspired by others. This becomes a creative conversation where we don't need to fight for our own ideas which we might already have settled on in advance. Neither will the conversation become a tool for reaching a preconceived goal.

The word *dialog* is often misused as a way of describing something which is not dialog at all. When we look at conversations between adults and children it is frightening to note how they often develop. More often than not the conversations are more like *interviews*. The adults ask some questions and the children might or might not answer these. It usually begins with a simple question: "How was your day at child care?" After a while the questions become nothing but a simple routine. The heart disappears and the questions soon become more controlling. Then the child will respond with a standard answer or cease to answer all together. This is a very limited conversation which neither person learns much from—they don't learn about themselves, the other person or their mutual relationship.

> *It is really important to ensure that there is a solid foundation in the adult relationship—also when the children are young. This way space will be created for dialog between adults and children. It also ensures that the relationship is open and honest, and that you continually work on the communication within the family.*

Parents need to make up their minds about which kind of language they want to use with their children; is it going to be an interview style or a conversation? This will make it easier to develop a dialog that will have a positive impact on the relationship with the children throughout their lives.

Prior to the 1970 parents had very different expectations to inter-generational family relationships than we have today. Since then, parents have more freely been able to make their own decisions regarding when to visit relatives. Many grandparents worry that their children might be sitting at home discussing how often they "have to" visit and if anyone can be exempt from going. When they finally turn up they might be staring at the clock as if all they are waiting for is to go home again. Some grandparents become rather depressed just by the thought of that. To prevent this when you become a grandparent it is important to ensure that a solid foundation is developed between you and your children—when they are young. You need to create space for dialog and ensure that the relationship is open and honest, and that your communication is based on equal dignity respecting each other's integrity. With an open communication like that you lay the foundation for a good relationship later in life where your children can meet you in a positive manner. This is much more important than anything various traditions, authorities, politicians and experts will tell you about setting limits, living up to expectations, controlling what children do, and so forth. Sure, you can set limits and follow traditions but you need to have a dialog about it. You need to give your children the opportunity to share and contribute with their own experiences.

—How do you develop a good and solid foundation for the relationship between parents and children? Are you able to give an example showing what parents can do?

—If the communication has been based on questions and instructions then it is really difficult to change the language when the children grow up. Dialog requires a completely different kind of openness which you cannot achieve through "Q&A conversations". That openness is necessary when our children make decisions that are challenging for us as parents. In situations like that it is beneficial to have experience with dialog. This enables you to openly explore where you are at rather than simply defining each other. When children do things that surprise their parents and perhaps upset their morals and ideals about etiquette it is a good idea not to rush to conclusions. Try instead to be open for dialog. You could say: "What you are saying (or did yesterday) is foreign to me. Are you able to tell me what you think? What made you do it?" By doing that you stay in contact with who your child is instead of only relating to what he/she has done. A dialog is a conversation based on equal dignity where both parties have equal value.

—The living room is often the space where we most easily become frustrated because it is a shared area. Some play the wrong music, some are noisy or messy, while others snatch each others things. The whole family should be able to share that room. Do you have any advice?

—Parents need to set the agenda and let everyone know what they want. It is all about *atmosphere* so it is once again more important *how* things are done than *what* is done. There are a number of different ways of watching television. Some adults would say that children are disobedient if they ask questions when the News in on. Watching television requires some people's full attention while others are able to chat while they watch. One person can feel terribly lonely even though the whole family is in the same room. Just like it is possible to feel connected when everyone is sitting in each their own rooms.

I meet parents with children between the ages of 14 and 17. They tell me that they haven't really spoken with their children since they were around eight or nine years old. This might explain why many children sit in their rooms watching television or playing computer games while their parents sit in the living room. When the family is together in one room without entertainment they don't know what to say to each other. If parents only ask children questions, they effectively hide behind the questions. They avoid having to expose themselves and their vulnerabilities, while the children are forced to answer and thereby expose themselves. This lack of equality enforces the distorted balance of power which already exists between parents and children. Add to this the fact that when you ask a question all you get is an answer. It doesn't give you any indication of what is on the child's mind. It is pure coincidence whether or not the question concerns anything of importance to the child. The one who asks takes away the positive energy from the relationship and the conversation, while the one who answers hands over their energy.

You can put this to the test. Every day you interview your partner about his day at work. You will soon realize how pointless it is. Besides, there is no substance in giving an account of what happened during the eight or more hours he has been at work. What really interests you is who he is and how he is feeling today.

It is important that each member of the family has the opportunity to share what is on their mind. This might be about what happened during the day or something completely different. It is not until we start talking about something that engages us that it becomes clear to others who we are. A conversation based on equal dignity is one where both parties are talking about themselves. Parents could think like this: "What would I say if it wasn't my son or daughter I was speaking with but my best friend?" Then you can say that instead. Maybe it is something you have thought about, someone you have met, holiday plans, whatever. You will notice that your child relaxes straight away. If you are able to do this two to three times a week then within a month the children will start talking about what is on their mind.

—It is not possible to have the same kind of dialog with all children. Some are rather shy and find it scary to tell a story. How is it possible to engage these children in a dialog? As parents we quickly resort to "the interview style" because children hardly say anything without being prompted.

—The best and most important thing you can do for these children is to encourage them to talk about themselves—about their day, experiences, stories and dreams. It isn't really important what they talk about but it is very important to make them feel at easy and that it is alright to say a few things. In that way they use their language. Behind their shyness often lies some kind of perfectionism which makes them fear. They fear that if they say everything which is on their mind it might sound stupid or they might get teased.

Some gentle inviting comment will be just fine, such as: "I know you feel shy but sometimes I am really curious to know what you are thinking . . ." Shyness is something parents need to deal with gently and carefully because it is very easy to make things worse by putting pressure on a shy child. Some, but not all, shy children enjoy playing theatre. They gain greater social confidence when they pretend to be someone else. *Shyness* is also a phenomenon which parents need to get used to and they need to learn to accept that this is the way their children are. Even though parents might think social relations are enjoyable they can be painful for the children.

—Often, I automatically ask my son "Yes!" and "No!" questions, but I don't get anything in return.

—That is what happens. These questions are fine when you need simple information but ideally you should consider *how* you ask the questions. Were you to ask your child everyday for six years about how their day was then you have yourself answered the question. Most children won't say anything if they didn't have a good day because that isn't what you want to hear. If you learn to ask *open-ended* questions you will be encouraging a much greater openness. Alternatively, you might need a bit of patience and wait until your child wants to tell you something. Building on your confidence and openness will be of great benefit to both you and your child. Your child will certainly start feeling that it is alright to be a bit different.

—But how do you build confidence? Does this happen by changing the questions? Instead of asking: "Are you alright?" I could ask: "How have you been?" Most parents probably want to build relationships on openness and trust but this is easier said than done.

—Sure! The latter way of asking is better than the former. "How have you been?" does not allow for a "Yes!" or a "No!" Most parents will have noticed that if they ask how their children have been, they will start talking about their day. Parent can also start talking about their day: "Today, I had to do so many difficult things . . ." or "Today, we had so much fun in the office . . ."

> *Most parents will have noticed that if they ask how their children have been, they will start talking about their day. Parent can also start talking about their day: "Today, I had to do so many difficult things . . ." or "Today, we had so much fun in the office . . ."*

There is no need to tell children what you are trying to achieve. You just need to start saying something instead of asking questions.

Then you display openness. You are *open* when you as a parent talk about your own thoughts and feelings. Tradition tells you that you are *self-obsessed* but this is not the case at all. The one who asks questions is closed and seen as being closed. Unless of course, you have a very animated body language which says something like: "Oh my goodness, did you really do that?!" This is different from asking routine questions such as: "How are you?", "How was school?", "How is you girlfriend?" and so forth.

—Children do not like those questions and when they are seven or eight years old they will most likely stop answering them. I understand why they think it is boring answering those questions.

—Adults don't like answering those questions either. The truth is that you are not asking your son what happened in his biology lesson because you are interested in biology. You are interested in his learning and well-being. You will get a much better insight into this if you let him tell you this himself.

My father died at home. The custom of our culture was that family, friends and neighbors would come and visit. I thought it was frustrating but my mother insisted on keeping the door open. I was in the living room and listened to her tell the same story over and over again. This served a purpose and was part of the grieving process. When you tell your story to someone else then a connection is formed. This does not happen if all you do is ask questions.

You only know how to raise children once they have grown up. You need to learn *with* your children and they know that frustration and mistakes are part of all learning. They forgive us, so it is alright to get angry—this won't harm the children.

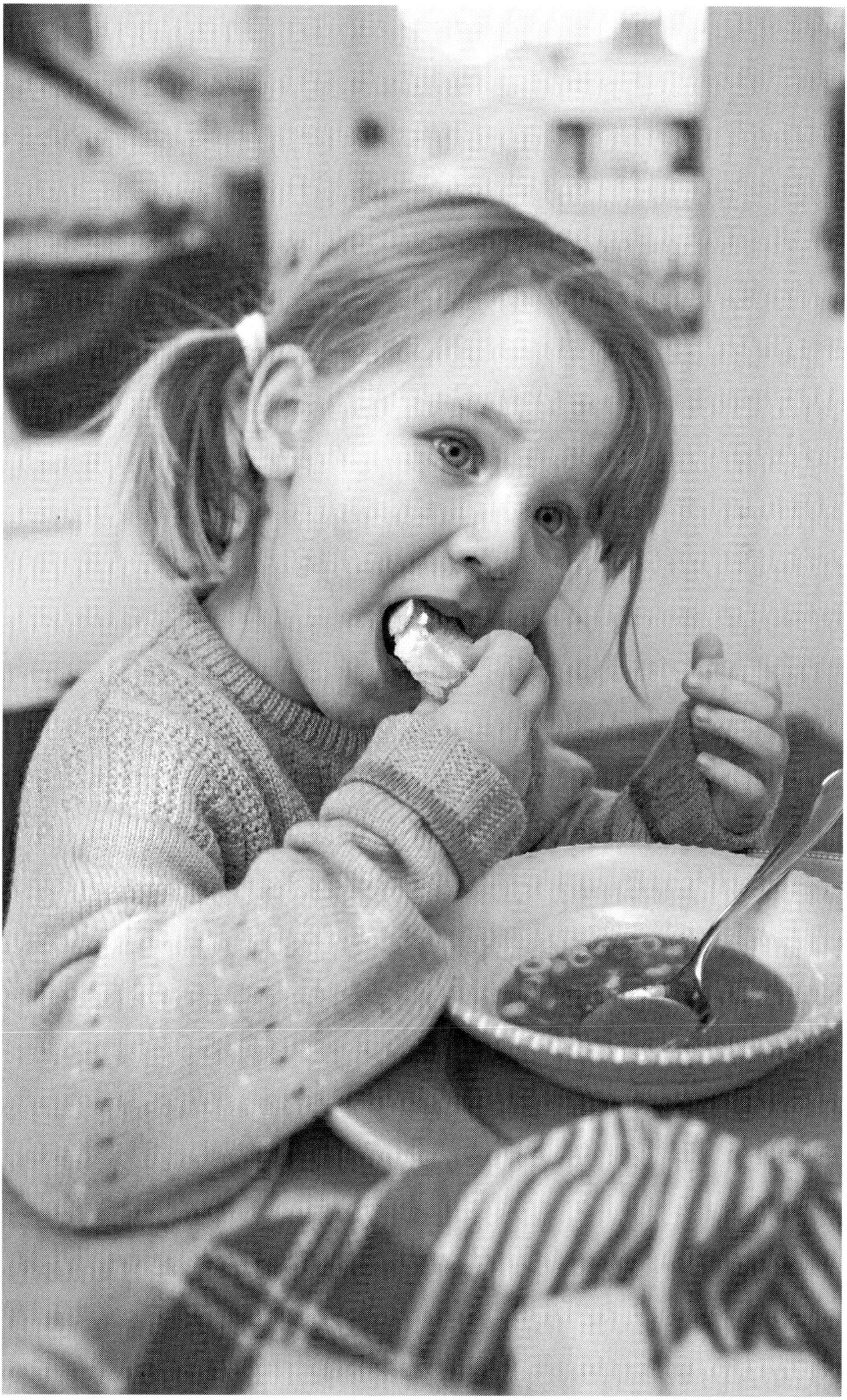

I am a journalist by heart and it is part of my nature to poke my nose in everything. I am curious. However, after reading some of Jesper's books I went home and started talking more about my day instead of always asking questions. I believe that this has lead to more open conversations and greater participation by all of us. It didn't happen straight away but it is happening. Every now and then someone might complain: "Do we always have to talk about everything?" and "Oh no! Do we have to begin another one of those deep and meaningful conversations?" I acknowledge that I have to find a balance so it doesn't turn into a burden but ensure that a comfortable atmosphere remains.

—Parents' conversations with children are often full of mistrust and morality. One of the parents might say: "You must remember that . . ." or "It is also important to . . ." Is it possible to become more constructive?

—When children hit puberty you can tell them that you no longer are a *law-maker*. You could say: "From now on I would like you to talk to yourself about important questions. Ask yourself if you think it is a good idea for you to buy a computer game. When you have thought about it for a few days you let me know what you think. You let me know what you have decided—if you have decided—and why?" Children have to find out whether or not they want to give themselves permission, and why?

If your son says: "I don't need to think about that because if I am allowed to decide then I will buy it!" In that situation you say: "This is not a question about who decides, neither is it a question about who is in charge. It is all about me beginning to share responsibility with you which is why I want you to think about it for a few days!" If he come back a few days later and says: "I have made up my mind, I do want to buy the computer game." Then you say: "Okay, how do you know that?" It is alright to tell him that his decision isn't justified properly. You can tell him that he must take your opinion seriously: "I will not prevent you from buying the game but I do want your decision to be better thought through than it is right now." You invite him to reflect and consider. He will be able to do this also when his is offered alcohol and drugs. Children need to practice making decisions based on what they think and feel—and not simply based on your morals.

> *It is important to teach children to ask themselves and to consider their personal values and experiences. It is all about becoming competent decision-makers—something they will need for the rest of their lives.*

Different families have different values and it will always be possible for your son to tell you about a number of his friends who are allowed to buy computer games. It is important to teach him to ask himself and to consider his personal values and experiences. This is not a question about parents handing over responsibility and letting their children do what they want. It is all about helping them become competent decision-makers—something they will need for the rest of their lives.

What happens if you seriously disagree with him and don't want him to buy the computer game? Should you stop him from buying it? No! You shouldn't go any further than to refuse funding the purchase. To stop him would be very unwise. To learn how to make good decisions requires that he makes some mistakes along the way. As an adult you need to allow him to do this. Sometimes he might not be able to foresee the consequences of his decisions. Then it is important for him to be able to have practiced his *inner dialog*. He might say: "I don't think I'm going to buy the computer game because I think you will be disappointed if I do." In that case you answer: "I might be disappointed but that is my problem. It is alright for you to think about the consequences and consider me but this must not be the deciding factor. You cannot live your life and base your decisions on what makes other people happy."

It might feel awkward saying this to your son because we are not used to dialog within families. In our society we traditionally only have debates or discussions. This is what it is like in politics. We sit in our couches and look on like the audience in a theatre. The politicians try to tear each other to pieces instead of getting together and talking about things like people with equal dignity. Afterwards, we don't know more about the topic or ourselves. When parents do what politicians do they become very poor role models.

I sense that many people believe life is passing and time is flying by. I feel that the days go quickly and we forget to be present and enjoy the moment. Some research shows that children have an inborn ability to meditate. They are able to let the imagination go free and give the brain a break—they do this much better than adults. Imagine if meditation could become part of child care, school and the daily routines at home? A contribution to an inner journey which calms the soul.

—What inspires children and young people in their aim for a harmonious and insightful life?

—I believe it is important to have parents who care about conversation and enjoy inspiration. Tell the children stories they can keep and remember five or ten years from now. My impression is that most people suffer from over-stimulation these days. I personally make sure I don't turn the music on in my living room. When I return home, especially after having worked in a big city, I need silence.

Family Time

Being with people all the time and often without much physical space is a serious stress-factor.

One reason why children in child care and schools are over-stimulated is because the carers and teachers are so good at what they do. Their job is to stimulate children. Many children are over-stimulated because they are forced into take part of social situations. This also stresses adults. Children almost become addicted to stimulation. When they come home they are restless and need calm but they are given more stimulation. Parents feel obliged to take over after the teachers. Then they start behaving like pseudo-teachers. Their children need to be entertained. It would be much better to say: "That is the end of your working day. Now you have time off!"

Today's children have lost something like 80 to 90% of the opportunity to choose when and how they want to be entertained. There is very little room for the silence which is necessary for being creative. Plenty of so-called "creative" activities happen all the time. They are painting, playing music, and so forth but that doesn't mean they are *creative*. Add to this that we live in an information society full of stimulation. It is hectic.

—*I know that this activity level also puts pressure on parents. Personally, I know it is good for me to be bored. I actually like it. Is it good for children just to sit with their thoughts and do "nothing"?*

—Children all over the world will sometimes go to their parents and say: "I am bored!" but the restlessness that the children feel are really *withdrawal symptoms*. Suddenly they don't have any external stimulation and then all they feel is *restlessness*. If they are able to put up with this for a maximum of 20 minutes the *creativity* kick in. So, when children are bored all you need to do is give them a friendly smile and say: "Good luck. It will be interesting to see what you come up with."

—Instead of telling them that it is good for them to be bored?

—You shouldn't say that. Most importantly, you shouldn't give them a long list of suggestions. This only limits their options. For generations parents have tried this and most of their suggestions have been rejected by children.

As adults we can ask ourselves: "How do I use my own energy and how do I recharge?" Daily routines alone suck a lot of energy out of children, so they also need some way of recharging. Most parents are surprised when I tell them that I spend hours everyday just staring out of the window. I am not bored but I work in silence. One of Denmark's most important coaches has told me that this is meditation. I also use a kind of meditative practice before I meet new people I need to relate to on a professional level. I empty my mind so I am able to meet them, not just without prejudice but also without knowledge. Only then am I able to learn something new. This has been very beneficial to me.

Introducing some sort meditation exercises in the home is a good idea. Teaching children how to deal with thoughts and feelings is excellent. Meditation and relaxation is not something you should start once problems arise. This should be done as a preventative measure to ensure general well-being. Parents might want to focus on the importance of relaxing or de-stressing. Instead of stopping at the fitness club on your way home from work you could go home and enjoy some relaxation exercises with your children. If you begin when the children are between 18 and 24 months old then you can do simple exercises where you put your hands on your stomach or chest—and your child does the same on his or her body. Then you slowly breathe in and out so that your stomach/chest rises. Talk about how this breathing gradually calms you down, and acknowledge how you both are able to relax your bodies.

Children can cope with a substantial amount of stress but they will not thrive unless they also learn how to relax. Many adults make a conscious effort to make sure they relax. They often start yoga, tai chi, pilate, art or meditation classes. For many it is important to be able to attend classes that are free of ideology and religion. You could argue that meditation is part of a Buddhist way of life but is just as much an old Christian tradition and indigenous peoples around the world have long practiced these techniques. Even very difficult children benefit greatly from practicing traditional breathing and relaxation exercises.

We ought to teach children how to listen to their inner voices.

You cannot simply say to children that everything will be fine if they just meditate for five minutes. Neither does it help telling them to: "Relax!" That's like a comment coming from a different universe. We take anti-depressants, consumer liters of alcohol, and do just about anything to calm our inner pain. Many people develop mental health problems and struggle with an inner unrest. Out of this has grown a massive and very profitable industry—especially the pharmaceutical industry—because we continually try to stifle and alleviate these pains. As a result we become highly stressed and will never get to know ourselves. Most people only chase more stimulation. We really ought to teach our children how to listen to their inner voice.

I often decide and control what is happening at home—I do this without being consciously aware of it. I think my parents did the same. I keep on doing it—no matter how hard it is to try not to. I am not even aware of it when it happens. I just repeat myself.

—*Why do we copy our parents and hang on to negative behavior—even though we deep down don't want it? If our parents were authoritarian we will also be authoritarian in spite of all our efforts. Why are we not able to break the cycle?*

—Children trust the way their parents love them. This means that the way our parents love us is the love we know—no matter how they did this. When most of us grew up it was sufficient for our parents to show loving feelings. These days we know that simply showing loving feelings is not enough. We need to convert those feelings into loving behavior. If your parents believed that an authoritarian upbringing with smacking and criticism was right—then that is what you think love is. In that way the cycle continues. If you are going to break this cycle you must first and foremost acknowledge that your parents were not perfect. For some this comes as a huge relief—for others it is serious challenge.

Even though we might say: "I would never do things like that to my children!" we do it anyway. Subconsciously, we copy behavior. There are two ways of noticing that this is happening:

1. When one of you suddenly says: "You are just like your father!" Most of us would see this as a criticism because the truth sometimes hurts and because we don't really want to be like our parents.
2. When you see yourself on video. It is often a shocking revelation for us to see how we behave.

Family Time

In the early days of my career as a family therapist I met a lady who was aware of how much she copied her father. He was a Church Minister and she thought she could simple break the cycle by leaving his Church. For some children, breaking with their parents' attitudes and ways of doing things is a rebellion of note—this might be political or religious. It is obvious that the lady needed to go much deeper if she really wanted to break the cycle. Otherwise, the problem would remain. The family who raises us teaches us how to love other people. This is one of the reasons why we have so many conflicts during the first 10 to 15 years of our relationships. It is most likely that we partner up with someone who has learned a different way of loving. When they love us, we don't feel loved—and the other way around. This is also the big difference between infatuation and love. Infatuation is deep and beautifully self-obsessed, whereas love requires us to work with the other person's conditions without letting go of our own.

—We say: "My" child, "my" husband and so forth. We assume a position where we "own" each other. People say: "These are my children and I decide what happens to them!" What does this indicate and tell us about our relationships?

—When you look at and relate to children like that you will sooner or later be punished. Within the family a number of issues will inevitably cause conflicts. If these conflicts become destructive and repeated more and more frequently and with an increasing negativity then parents need to start doing things differently. More often than not this means that it is about time the parents hand over some of the responsibility to their children.

The so called "experts" and politicians have been saying that parents in general should be more responsible and focus more on *upbringing*. It is wrong to think that *upbringing* happens when parents consciously try to do this by deciding, controlling and directing their children. The truth is that what adults call *upbringing* has no effect whatsoever. It simply goes in one ear and out the other. *Upbringing* is what happens between the lines.

How does a child learn about dealing with conflicts? Simple: they learn by watching and observing how their parents do it. It doesn't make sense to tell children to speak nicely to each other if their parents don't do it to each other. Children don't do as we say—they do as we do. It is my opinion that children these days get far too much *upbringing*. Parents are far to focused on making sure their children behave in one way or another. They listen to all sorts of experts, and are preoccupied with being perfect.

> *Upbringing is what happens between the lines. How does a child learn about dealing with conflicts? Simple: they learn by watching and observing how their parents do it. It doesn't make sense to tell children to speak nicely to each other if their parents don't do it to each other.*

Instead of deciding over their children, parents ought to hand over some of the responsibility to them and stop behaving as if they own them. All children are essentially diplomatic by nature but they will turn up the volume if we don't listens to them. Then they will become challenging—especially teenagers—simply because they feel ignored. I once wanted to watch a movie on the television. My son was 11 years old and wanted to watch it as well but it didn't start until 11 pm. The morning after he had to sit a test at school and without thinking twice about it both his mother and I said: "Don't you think you should go to bed early considering you have to sit the test tomorrow morning?" With a smile he said: "The real question is whether or not you should continue questioning my bed time?"

—*Wow!*

—It was very diplomatic. So we said: "Alright, sorry about that!" He watched the movie for a little while and went to bed. Your children, and every child, will do exactly the same. As long as they are not under duress they will work it out for themselves. Had I said to him that I thought it would be a stupid idea to watch the movie he would have wanted to watch it from start to finish—he would have become obstinate. Instead he was able to follow his own intuition. This is a new kind of *parental leadership*. Unfortunately, parents are told by "experts" that things need to be done certain ways. This is not necessarily so. You can simply say: "Right, during the past 11 years I have made sure you got enough sleep. I have enjoyed this responsibility but now it is your turn. I know you can handle it but I am not so sure I can. From time to time I will most likely tell you to go to bed—please just ignore that."

The fact that children no longer have any *adult free* time or space is without doubt a tragic consequence of the societal changes during the past 30 years. It is indeed a great shame that they can no longer play anywhere without adults being present. Once upon a time children developed their social competencies through play and communication with other children. They no longer have that opportunity as there is always an adult nearby who will interfere with what is happening. The adults are usually also rather idealistic and romantic, and will not tolerate conflicts. These days it is not particularly enjoyable being a child with adults hanging around all the time. Add to this the fact that adults are discussing how important it is to set limits for children. This is unbelievable because children have never been as restricted as they are now. Adults are involved and controlling everything children do. They consequently have limited opportunities for finding out who they are and developing from the inside at their own pace. From when I was seven until puberty I mixed with other children of all ages and both girls and boys. Today, they are more often that not divided up into like-minded, age similar and gender specific groups. This obviously has an impact on their abilities to interact and learn.

—What does happen to them? What happens to their image of self when their mother or father constantly watch over them and interfere with everything they do?

—They become seriously insecure and will lack essential life skills. They only know how to rely on adult experiences. The fact is that children are capable of doing many things by themselves—but that doesn't mean they should be left to do them on their own. They might come to you and say: "It is getting really late and I am worried that I won't wake up early enough tomorrow morning. Do you mind waking me up?" This means it is the child's responsibility to ask for help. It isn't you as a parent who should tell them that they need help. *Deciding* and *being allowed to* are terms related to power. We need to give our children responsibility. You might give them some clear choices that are age appropriate, not because you cannot make up your mind but out of courtesy. Then they will be given the opportunity to do things by themselves—but not alone.

This is the key challenge when developing new adult leadership. When children start to question who decides—then they are old enough to take responsibility.

—I have noticed that many children are overly responsible. They behave almost like adults, and are preoccupied with satisfying adults. How should their parents deal with that?

—That depends on the relationship you have with these children. If you don't have a really close family then I don't think you should get involved. They don't need any kind of criticism. They need support so they can assume greater responsibility for themselves. Then they won't be overly responsible. You could say: "It is great that you want to help me but isn't there something else you would rather do?" When children are unable to express themselves and take responsibility for themselves they need a gentle invitation. They need someone who sees the good in them. It is similar to adults who are inhibited in relation to sexual intercourse. They don't like to get undressed while their partner is looking. If they are to relax in relation to their sexuality then they need many gentle invitations before they feel comfortable. Just like children who feel alone and find it difficult to express themselves. They need to be invited by people who are genuinely interested. Not by people who control them, correct them, think they do things wrong or believe they have a problem.

The other day my son came home a told me about a new pocket money arrangement his father and bonus mother had implemented: During the week he has the responsibility for planning and carrying out two projects: wash his clothes and prepare dinner one evening. "Brilliant!" I thought.

I often feel that we as parents take initiative, come up with ideas and dreams. It is difficult to make all of it happen. Much of this is driven by our desires. Neither parents nor children find it terribly exciting doing the dishes and tidying but it has to be done.

—A family of five consists of two adults and three children of varying ages—all with different needs. Let's say it is Saturday and the family is together. How is it possible to ensure everyone has a good day?

—I believe the family could do this exactly like a couple would, namely by talking about it. You just need to make sure you remember the difference between *needs* and *wants*. Children mostly focus on what they *want*. With your position of leadership you know that the family has *needs*. You could take turns and let everyone express what they would like to do. Then you could say: "Alright, here we have five wishes that will be difficult to combine. I would really like all of us to do something together. Will that be possible?" Then you need to discuss things back and forth.

It is often less important for the children to get what they want as long as they experience that they are listened to and taken seriously. All of us feel like that, really. Democracy is not about everybody getting what they want but about everybody being taken seriously. Everybody needs to get as much as possible of what they would like. If a six to eight year old rarely wants to do anything with the rest of the family then there is something wrong with the atmosphere.

Sometimes parents need to think a few steps ahead to make sure they don't end up with serious conflicts. I will not ask my grandson: "Alex, do you feel like going for a walk?" I say: "Alex, let's go for a walk!" If he doesn't want to he can just say: "No!" He is given a choice but I am not holding him responsible for it. Children don't often *feel like* going for walks. You live up to your responsibilities as a leader when you present your ideas and say: "What do you think of this?" If someone says: "I would rather do something else!" and you say: "We are going to do what I said!" then you are not a good leader. This is not about making children responsible for the choices, but about giving them the freedom to say: "Yes!" or "No!" It is a good idea to ask children: "What do you want to do?"

—*Instead of asking them: "What would you like to do?"*

—No, that's not a good question. If you have been asked what you *want to do* for your entire life then you are able to distinguish between what you *want* and what you *would like*. We very often have to do things we don't *like* doing to be able to achieve what we *want*. Children might not *like* doing homework but this is necessary if they want to go to university. A person who only follows spontaneous desires without reflecting on possible consequences is called a psychopath.

> *If you have been asked what you "want to do" for your entire life then you are able to distinguish between what you "want" and what you "would like". Very often we have to do things we don't like doing to be able to achieve what we "want".*

Employers are pulling their hair out because recent generations have been taught that their world is all about what they *like* doing. They do not accept that "No!" can in fact mean "No!" Neither are they used to doing things just because they have to be done. It is like that with children. If they continually are being asked what they *would like* to do then they will go through long periods of time when they will no longer talk about what they *would like* but instead focus on what they *don't like*. That seriously drains everyone's energy. In the end children will no longer know what they do want and become insecure.

Many adults know that it is essential for them to say what they *want* if they want a good relationship. We need to be able to know the difference between what we *want* and what we *would like*. This is difficult for some women because we have a long tradition of men's *wants* setting the agenda. This is why some women see themselves as authoritarian or self-centered when they start saying what they *want*. It is perfectly alright if you would *like* to do something but that should not determine what the family does—what we *want* is most important.

We have previously spoken about sons and adult men who are not able to say: "No!" to their mothers. This frustrates them greatly—and it makes their wives lonely. There is something very important boys should learn from their fathers, namely to say: "No!" to women. If a women says to her husband: "I would like to go shopping today, would you like to come?" Then it is alright for him to say: "I would like to come to town but not to go shopping." When the son hears his father say that he will learn something highly valuable. He learns how he can say what he wants. He learns how to say it without getting into a fight and without using his *power of definition* which he would have done had he said: "All you want to do is shop, shop, shop. It is ridiculous!" Every negotiation ought to be about everyone stating what they want to do. When that happens we start realizing that doing what we would like is no longer as important as doing something together.

—*How can we deal with that as a family?*

—By letting the whole family talk and listen for as long as it takes for everyone to understand each other's needs and wants. We must spend time together. The family and the rapport between the adults and children are more important than work, spare time and hobbies. The interactions and communications within the family form the basis for how we develop—and who we become.

> *We must spend time together. The family and the rapport between the adults and children are more important than work, spare time and hobbies. The interactions and communications within the family form the basis for how we develop—and who we become.*

A FINAL WORD
– The role of *values* within the home

We use the term *values* about something which would really be described more accurately as *a set of guiding principles*.

Values are tangible and often refer to wealth that can be defined by some kind of financial value. *A set of guiding principles* however, play an important role as a compass when we enter into conflicts and need to make decisions. This issue has become relevant because we no longer have a consensus of values in our society. Raising children and living together is often based on random knowledge which is not put into the context of our shared values. If we do not have *a set of guiding principles* within the family we will live from conflict to conflict and life will be hectic indeed. If you do not have a compass to help you navigate you could end up anywhere.

I have endeavored to write about four *fundamental values*. In my experience these are a constructive *set of guiding principles* for the interactions between adults, and between adults and children. These are:

- Equal dignity
- Authenticity
- Integrity
- Personal responsibility

I trust this will inspire you—please don't blindly copy these. Instead I encourage you to consider the four *fundamental values* carefully so you are able to understand which values you bring with you from your own childhood—and which your partner brings. How do these values supplement each other? How are they contradictory? Regardless of which conditions and values you decide to incorporate, it is important that you decide on some. It will make life a lot easier!

Jesper Juul

family/lab

WE MAKE GOOD FAMILIES BETTER

FamilyLab operates as a "Laboratory" where professionals, educators, parents and children work together to find new ways of transforming emotional love and commitment into loving behaviour. **FamilyLab** is therefore a constantly evolving organisation, always focussed on the relationships between people.

We believe there are better ways to raise and educate children than using authoritarian force or democratic tricks. Instead we embrace relationships based on equal dignity, authenticity, integrity and self-responsibility.

FamilyLab is actively supporting the health and well-being of today's parents/educators and tomorrow's children through a series of seminars and workshops. We participate in public debate and policy development with the aim of creating an optimal environment for reciprocal social, emotional and educational learning.

If you would like further information, and to be at the forefront of this exiting paradigm shift, please visit our website where you can book a speaker or sign up for a seminar or workshop. You can also purchase books, DVDs, articles, interviews, Q&A and family coaching transcripts.

All of our materials deal with issues that are part of most families' and educators' daily lives. They are easy to read and full of practical ideas, looking at new ways of developing relationships with children.

www.family-lab.com | www.familylab.com.au
www.jesperjuul.com | www.zentv.se

Other Jesper Juul Books at AuthorHouse:

978-1-4685-7931-4

NO!
The art of saying No! with a clear conscience

This might be the most decisive book you can find in terms of defining your relationship with your partner, children, parents, siblings and close friends.

Jesper Juul reveals with great insight why it is only possible to say "Yes!" to yourself when you also feel liberated and free to say "No!" to others. By letting go of the obligation to be nice and the need to serve and please others, it is easier to connect with your true identity. Jesper Juul reveals the secret to developing and maintaining a healthy mind, social competence as well as staying true to yourself.

When reading this practical book you will discover why "No!" is also called "the most loving answer" and therefore is the ultimate gift to yourself and those you hold near and dear.

978-1-4685-7933-8

"HERE I AM!" "WHO ARE YOU?"
Resolving conflicts between adults and children.

In this excellent, short and instructive book - maybe one of Jesper Juul's best - he explains how to handle yourself as an adult in conflict with children. The many ideas, concepts and practical suggestions apply whether you are a parent or a professional working in the educational system.

The title summarizes the essence of true dialogue and through plenty of everyday examples this book provides adults with alternatives to shouting, criticizing and blaming - while respecting the personal integrity of everyone involved.

Jesper Juul shows how to use personal language and thereby develop relationships built on equal dignity. Ultimately, this book helps adults become more authentic so children can be treated as real people.

978-1-4685-7927-7

FAMLY LIFE
The most important values for living together and raising children

This book captures the essence of modern family life. Much has changed since our own childhoods; "the good old days". Today's parents are challenged by the need to invent their own parenting style. This can only happen from within, based on our personal values and boundaries.

Jesper Juul puts it very clearly: "The love we feel for our children and our partners does not in itself have any value. It has no value at all until it is converted into loving behavior."

Each chapter focuses on the values that form a solid platform on which to build a family: Equal dignity, Integrity, Authenticity and Responsibility. This makes family life more meaningful and parents avoid living frantically from conflict to conflict, desperately searching for quick solutions and trying to adapt to the most popular parenting technique of the day. A book full of everyday examples and practical ideas.

978-1-4772-2602-5

DO WE REALLY NEED STRONG AND HEALTHY CHILDREN?

In this essay Jesper Juul is asking not only parents but also institutions, policy-makers and experts to take a serious look at what they want with our children and youth because rhetoric and practice seem to contradictive. Jesper Juul is also making clear what a strong and healthy child is and the enormous impact it would have on our societies if we decided to prioritize mental and social health.

WOMAN & MOTHER

In this essay Jesper JuuJ is investigating the role and self-image of women and mothers and expresses his worries that pat of women's mindset as well as behavior is self-destructive. The central section for parents is called "What really happens to nice girls" where the author is challenging our present values related to the education and upbringing of girls and young.

RAISING COMPETENT CHILDREN
The ANZ & USA edition of the European bestseller,
"Your Competent Child"

It is full of inspiration on how to raise competent children and how to develop relationships based on equal dignity, integrity and authenticity, and how to allow your children to develop self-responsibility - both personal and social.

Raising Competent Children is easy to read and draws on examples from everyday life. "Jesper Juul is one of the twelve leading enlighteners, thinkers and visionaries." Die ZEIT Germany's largest weekly newspaper.

Printed in Great Britain
by Amazon